1.35

# KEITH OF THE BORDER

# Keith of the Border

## A TALE OF THE PLAINS

*by*

### RANDALL PARRISH

AUTHOR *of* MY LADY *of* THE SOUTH
WHEN WILDERNESS WAS KING, ETC., ETC.

WITH FOUR
ILLUSTRATIONS IN FULL COLOR
*by*
W. HERBERT DUNTON

CHICAGO
A. C. McCLURG & CO.
1910

# CONTENTS

# CONTENTS

# ILLUSTRATIONS

# KEITH OF THE BORDER

## A TALE OF THE PLAINS

### CHAPTER I

#### THE PLAINSMAN

THE man was riding just below the summit of the ridge, occasionally uplifting his head so as to gaze across the crest, shading his eyes with one hand, to thus better concentrate his vision. Both horse and rider plainly exhibited signs of weariness, but every movement of the latter showed ceaseless vigilance, his glance roaming the barren ridges, a brown Winchester lying cocked across the saddle pommel, his left hand taut on the rein. Yet the horse he bestrode scarcely required restraint, advancing slowly, with head hanging low, and only occasionally breaking into a brief trot under the impetus of the spur.

The rider was a man approaching thirty, somewhat slender and long of limb, but possessing broad, squared shoulders above a deep chest, sitting the saddle easily in plainsman fashion, yet with an erectness of carriage

9

which suggested military training. The face under the wide brim of the weather-worn slouch hat was clean-shaven, browned by sun and wind, and strongly marked, the chin slightly prominent, the mouth firm, the gray eyes full of character and daring. His dress was that of rough service, plain leather " chaps," showing marks of hard usage, a gray woolen shirt turned low at the neck, with a kerchief knotted loosely about the sinewy bronzed throat. At one hip dangled the holster of a " forty-five," on the other hung a canvas-covered canteen. His was figure and face to be noted anywhere, a man from whom you would expect both thought and action, and one who seemed to exactly fit into his wild environment.

Where he rode was the very western extreme of the prairie country, billowed like the sea, and from off the crest of its higher ridges, the wide level sweep of the plains was visible, extending like a vast brown ocean to the foothills of the far-away mountains. Yet the actual commencement of that drear, barren expanse was fully ten miles distant, while all about where he rode the conformation was irregular, comprising narrow valleys and swelling mounds, with here and there a sharp ravine, riven from the rock, and invisible until one drew up startled at its very brink. The general trend of depression was undoubtedly southward, leading toward the valley of the Arkansas, yet irregular ridges occasionally cut across, adding to the confusion. The entire surrounding landscape presented the same aspect, with no special object upon which the eye could rest for guidance — no tree, no upheaval of rock, no peculiarity of summit, no snake-like trail,— all about extended the same dull, dead monotony of brown, sun-baked hills, with slightly greener depressions lying between, interspersed by patches of sand or the white gleam of alkali. It was a dreary, deserted land, parched under the hot summer sun, brightened by no vegetation, excepting sparse bunches of buffalo grass or an occasional stunted sage bush, and disclosing nowhere slightest sign of human habitation.

The rising sun reddened the crest of the hills, and the rider, halting his willing horse, sat motionless, gazing steadily into the southwest. Apparently he perceived nothing there unusual, for he slowly turned his body about in the saddle, sweeping his eyes, inch by inch, along the line of the horizon, until the entire circuit had been completed. Then his compressed lips smiled slightly, his hand unconsciously patting the horse's neck.

" I reckon we 're still alone, old girl," he said quietly, a bit of Southern drawl in the voice. " We 'll try for the trail, and take it easy."

He swung stiffly out of the saddle, and with reins

dangling over his shoulder, began the slower advance on foot, the exhausted horse trailing behind.  His was not a situation in which one could feel certain of safety, for any ridge might conceal the wary foemen he sought to avoid, yet he proceeded now with renewed confidence.  It was the Summer of 1868, and the place the very heart of the Indian country, with every separate tribe ranging between the Yellowstone and the Brazos, either restless or openly on the war-path. Rumors of atrocities were being retold the length and breadth of the border, and every report drifting in to either fort or settlement only added to the alarm.  For once at least the Plains Indians had discovered a common cause, tribal differences had been adjusted in war against the white invader, and Kiowas, Comanches, Arapahoes, Cheyennes, and Sioux, had become welded together in savage brotherhood.  To oppose them were the scattered and unorganized settlers lining the more eastern streams, guarded by small detachments of regular troops posted here and there amid that broad wilderness, scarcely within touch of each other.

Everywhere beyond these lines of patrol wandered roaming war parties, attacking travellers on the trails, raiding exposed settlements, and occasionally venturing to try open battle with the small squads of armed men. In this stress of sudden emergency — every available soldier on active duty — civilians had been pressed into service, and hastily despatched to warn exposed settlers, guide wagon trains, or carry despatches between outposts. And thus our rider, Jack Keith, who knew every foot of the plains lying between the Republican and the Canadian Rivers, was one of these thus suddenly requisitioned, merely because he chanced to be discovered unemployed by the harassed commander of a cantonment just without the environs of Carson City. Twenty minutes later he was riding swiftly into the northwest, bearing important news to General Sheridan, commander of the Department, who happened at that moment to be at Fort Cairnes. To Keith this had been merely another page in a career of adventure; for him to take his life in his hands had long ago become an old story. He had quietly performed the special duty allotted him, watched a squadron of troopers trot forth down the valley of the Republican, received the hasty thanks of the peppery little general, and then, having nothing better to do, traded his horse in at the government corral for a fresh mount and started back again for Carson City. For the greater portion of two nights and a day he had been in the saddle, but he was accustomed to this, for he had driven more than one bunch of longhorns up the Texas trail; and as he had slept three hours at Cairnes, and as his nerves were like steel, the thought of danger gave him slight concern. He was thoroughly tired, and it rested him to get out of the saddle, while the freshness of the morning air was a tonic, the very breath of which made him forgetful of fatigue.

After all, this was indeed the very sort of experience which appealed to him, and always had — this life of peril in the open, under the stars and the sky. He had constantly experienced it for so long now, eight years, as to make it seem merely natural. While he ploughed steadily forward through the shifting sand of the coulee, his thought drifted idly back over those years, and sometimes he smiled, and occasionally frowned, as various incidents returned to memory. It had been a rough life, yet one not unusual to those of his generation. Born of excellent family in tidewater Virginia, his father a successful planter, his mother had died while he was still in early boyhood, and he had grown up cut off from all womanly influence. He had barely attained his majority, a senior at William and Mary's College, when the Civil War came; and one month after Virginia cast in her lot with the South, he became a sergeant in a cavalry regiment commanded by his father. He had enjoyed that life and won his spurs, yet it had cost. There was much not over pleasant to remember, and those strenuous years of almost ceaseless fighting, of long night marches, of swift, merciless raiding, of lonely scouting within the enemy's lines, of severe wounds, hardship, and suffering, had left their marks on both body and soul. His father had fallen on the field at Antietam, and left him utterly alone in the world, but he had fought on grimly to the end, until the last flag of the Confederacy had been furled. By that time, upon the collar of his tattered gray jacket appeared the tarnished insignia of a captain. The quick tears dimmed his eyes even now as he recalled anew that final parting following Appomattox, the battle-worn faces of his men, and his own painful journey homeward, defeated, wounded, and penniless. It was no home when he got there, only a heap of ashes and a few weed-grown acres. No familiar face greeted him; not even a slave was left.

He had honestly endeavored to remain there, to face the future and work it out alone; he persuaded himself to feel that this was his paramount duty to the State, to the memory of the dead. But those very years of army life made such a task impossible; the dull, dead monotony of routine, the loneliness, the slowness of results, became intolerable. As it came to thousands of his comrades, the call of the West came to him, and at last he yielded, and drifted toward the frontier. The life there fascinated him, drawing him deeper and deeper into its swirling vortex. He became freighter,

mail carrier, hunter, government scout, cowboy, fore-
man. Once he had drifted into the mountains, and took
a chance in the mines, but the wide plains called him
back once more to their desert loneliness. What an utter
waste it all seemed, now that he looked back upon it.
Eight years of fighting, hardship, and rough living, and
what had they brought him? The reputation of a hard
rider, a daring player at cards, a quick shot, a scorner
of danger, and a bad man to fool with — that was
the whole of a record hardly won. The man's eyes
hardened, his lips set firmly, as this truth came crush-
ing home. A pretty life story surely, one to be proud
of, and with probably no better ending than an Indian
bullet, or the flash of a revolver in some barroom fight.

The narrow valley along which he was travelling suddenly changed its direction, compelling him to climb
the rise of the ridge. Slightly below the summit he
halted. In front extended the wide expanse of the
Arkansas valley, a scene of splendor under the golden
rays of the sun, with vivid contrast of colors, the gray
of rocks, the yellow of sand, the brown of distant hills,
the green of vegetation, and the silver sheen of the
stream half hidden behind the fringe of cottonwoods
lining its banks. This was a sight Keith had often
looked upon, but always with appreciation, and for the
moment his eyes swept across from bluff to bluff with-

out thought except for its wild beauty. Then he perceived something which instantly startled him into attention — yonder, close beside the river, just beyond that ragged bunch of cottonwoods, slender spirals of blue smoke were visible. That would hardly be a camp of freighters at this hour of the day, and besides, the Santa Fé trail along here ran close in against the bluff, coming down to the river at the ford two miles further west. No party of plainsmen would ever venture to build a fire in so exposed a spot, and no small company would take the chances of the trail. But surely that appeared to be the flap of a canvas wagon top a little to the right of the smoke, yet all was so far away he could not be certain. He stared in that direction a long while, shading his eyes with both hands, unable to decide. There were three or four moving black dots higher up the river, but so far away he could not distinguish whether men or animals. Only as outlined against the yellow sand dunes could he tell they were advancing westward toward the ford.

Decidedly puzzled by all this, yet determined to solve the mystery and unwilling to remain hidden there until night, Keith led his horse along the slant of the ridge, until he attained a sharp break through the bluff leading down into the valley. It was a rugged gash, nearly impassable, but a half hour of toil won them the lower

2

prairie, the winding path preventing the slightest view of what might be meanwhile transpiring below. Once safely out in the valley the river could no longer be seen, while barely a hundred yards away, winding along like a great serpent, ran the deeply rutted trail to Santa Fé. In neither direction appeared any sign of human life. As near as he could determine from those distant cottonwoods outlined against the sky, for the smoke spirals were too thin by then to be observed, the spot sought must be considerably to the right of where he had emerged. With this idea in mind he advanced cautiously, his every sense alert, searching anxiously for fresh signs of passage or evidence of a wagon train having deserted the beaten track, and turned south. The trail itself, dustless and packed hard, revealed nothing, but some five hundred yards beyond the ravine he discovered what he sought — here two wagons had turned sharply to the left, their wheels cutting deeply enough into the prairie sod to show them heavily laden. With the experience of the border he was able to determine that these wagons were drawn by mules, two span to each, their small hoofs clearly defined on the turf, and that they were being driven rapidly, on a sharp trot as they turned, and then, a hundred feet further, at a slashing gallop. Just outside their trail appeared the marks of a galloping horse.

A few rods farther along Keith came to a confused blur of pony tracks sweeping in from the east, and the whole story of the chase was revealed as though he had witnessed it with his own eyes. They must have been crazy, or else impelled by some grave necessity, to venture along this trail in so small a party. And they were travelling west — west! Keith drew a deep breath, and swore to himself, " Of all the blame fools! "

He perceived the picture in all its grewsome details — the two mule-drawn wagons moving slowly along the trail in the early morning; the band of hostile Indians suddenly swooping out from some obscure hiding place in the bluffs; the discovery of their presence; the desperate effort at escape; the swerving from the open trail in vain hope of reaching the river and finding protection underneath its banks; the frightened mules galloping wildly, lashed into frenzy by the man on horseback; the pounding of the ponies' hoofs, punctuated by the exultant yells of the pursuers. Again he swore:

" Of all the blame fools! "

# CHAPTER II

## THE SCENE OF TRAGEDY

WHATEVER might be the nature of the tragedy it would be over with long before this, and those moving black spots away yonder to the west, that he had discerned from the bluff, were undoubtedly the departing raiders. There was nothing left for Keith to do except determine the fate of the unfortunates, and give their bodies decent burial. That any had escaped, or yet lived, was altogether unlikely, unless, perchance, women had been in the party, in which case they would have been borne away prisoners.

Confident that no hostiles would be left behind to observe his movements, Keith pressed steadily forward, leading his horse. He had thus traversed fully half a mile before coming upon any evidence of a fight — here the pursuers had apparently come up with the wagons, and circled out upon either side. From their ponies' tracks there must have been a dozen in the band. Perhaps a hundred yards further along lay two dead ponies. Keith examined them closely — both had been ridden with saddles, the marks of the cinches plainly visible.

Evidently one of the wagon mules had also dropped in the traces here, and had been dragged along by his mates. Just beyond came a sudden depression in the prairie down which the wagons had plunged so heavily as to break one of the axles; the wheel lay a few yards away, and, somewhat to the right, there lay the wreck of the wagon itself, two dead mules still in the traces, the vehicle stripped of contents and charred by fire. A hundred feet farther along was the other wagon, its tongue broken, the canvas top ripped open, while between the two were scattered odds and ends of wearing apparel and provisions, with a pile of boxes smoking grimly. The remaining mules were gone, and no semblance of life remained anywhere. Keith dropped his reins over his horse's head, and, with Winchester cocked and ready, advanced cautiously.

Death from violence had long since become almost a commonplace occurrence to Keith, yet now he shrank for an instant as his eyes perceived the figure of a man lying motionless across the broken wagon tongue. The grizzled hair and beard were streaked with blood, the face almost unrecognizable, while the hands yet grasped a bent and shattered rifle. Evidently the man had died fighting, beaten down by overwhelming numbers after expending his last shot. Then those fiends had scalped and left him where he fell. Fifty feet beyond, shot in the back, lay a younger man, doubled up in a heap, also scalped and dead. That was all; Keith scouted over a wide circle, even scanning the stretch of gravel under the river bank, before he could fully satisfy himself there were no others in the party. It seemed impossible that these two travelling alone would have ventured upon such a trip in the face of known Indian hostility. Yet they must have done so, and once again his lips muttered:

" Of all the blame fools ! "

Suddenly he halted, staring about over the prairie, obsessed by a new thought, an aroused suspicion. There had appeared merely the hoof-prints of the one horse alongside of the fleeing wagons when they first turned out from the trail, and that horse had been newly shod. But there were two dead ponies lying back yonder; neither shod, yet both had borne saddles. More than this, they had been spurred, the blood marks still plainly visible, and one of them was branded; he remembered it now, a star and arrow. What could all this portend? Was it possible this attack was no Indian affair after all? Was the disfiguring of bodies, the scalping, merely done to make it appear the act of savages? Driven to investigation by this suspicion, he passed again over the trampled ground, marking this time every separate indentation, every faintest imprint

of hoof or foot.   There was no impression of a mocca-
sin anywhere; every mark remaining was of booted
feet.   The inference was sufficiently plain — this had
been the deed of white men, not of red; foul murder,
and not savage war.

The knowledge seemed to seer Keith's brain with
fire, and he sprang to his feet, hands clinched and eyes
blazing.   He could have believed this of Indians, it
was according to their nature, their method of warfare;
but the cowardliness of it, the atrocity of the act, as
perpetrated by men of his own race, instantly aroused
within him a desire for vengeance.   He wanted to run
the fellows down, to discover their identity.   Without
thinking of personal danger, he ran forward on their
trail, which led directly westward, along the line of
cottonwoods.   These served to conceal his own movements, yet for the moment, burning with passion, he
was utterly without caution, without slightest sense of
peril.   He must know who was guilty of such a crime;
he felt capable of killing them even as he would ven-
omous snakes.   It was a perfectly plain trail to follow,
for the fugitives, apparently convinced of safety, and
confident their cowardly deed would be charged to Indian raiders, had made no particular effort at concealment, but had ridden away at a gallop, their horses'
hoofs digging deeply into the soft turf.   On this re-

treat they had followed closely along the river bank, aiming for the ford, and almost before he realized it Keith was himself at the water's edge where the trail abruptly ended, staring vaguely across toward the opposite shore. Even as he stood there, realizing the futility of further pursuit amid the maze of sand dunes opposite, the sharp reports of two rifles reached him, spurts of smoke rose from the farther bank, and a bullet chugged into the ground at his feet, while another sang shrilly overhead.

These shots, although neither came sufficiently near to be alarming, served to send Keith to cover. Coolheaded and alert now, his first mad rage dissipated, he scanned the opposite bank cautiously, but could nowhere discover any evidence of life. Little by little he comprehended the situation, and decided upon his own action. The fugitives were aware of his presence, and would prevent his crossing the stream, yet they were not at all liable to return to this side and thus reveal their identity. To attempt any further advance would be madness, but he felt perfectly secure from molestation so long as he remained quietly on the north shore. Those shots were merely a warning to keep back; the very fact that the men firing kept concealed was proof positive that they simply wished to be left alone. They were not afraid of what he knew now, only desirous

of not being seen. Confident as to this, he retreated
openly, without making the slightest effort to conceal
his movements, until he had regained the scene of murder. In evidence of the truth of his theory no further
shots were fired, and although he watched that opposite sand bank carefully, not the slightest movement
revealed the presence of others. That every motion
he made was being observed by keen eyes he had no
doubt, but this knowledge did not disconcert him, now
that he felt convinced fear of revealment would keep
his watchers at a safe distance. Whoever they might
be they were evidently more anxious to escape discovery
than he was fearful of attack, and possessed no desire
to take his life, unless it became necessary to prevent
recognition. They still had every reason to believe
their attack on the wagons would be credited to hostile Indians, and would consider it far safer to remain
concealed, and thus harbor this supposition. They
could not suspect that Keith had already stumbled upon
the truth, and was determined to verify it.

Secure in this conception of the situation, yet still
keeping a wary eye about to guard against any treachery, the plainsman, discovering a spade in the nearest
wagon, hastily dug a hole in the sand, wrapped the dead
bodies in blankets, and deposited them therein, piling
above the mound the charred remains of boxes as some

slight protection against prowling wolves. He searched the clothing of the men, but found little to reward the effort, a few letters which were slipped into his pockets to be read later, some ordinary trinkets hardly worth preserving except that they might assist in identifying the victims, and, about the neck of the elder man, a rather peculiar locket, containing a portrait painted on ivory. Keith was a long time opening this, the spring being very ingeniously concealed, but upon finally succeeding, he looked upon the features of a woman of middle age, a strong mature face of marked refinement, exceedingly attractive still, with smiling dark eyes, and a perfect wealth of reddish brown hair. He held the locket open in his hands for several minutes, wondering who she could be, and what possible connection she could have held with the dead. Something about that face smiling up into his own held peculiar fascination for him, gripping him with a strange feeling of familiarity, touching some dim memory which failed to respond. Surely he had never seen the original, for she was not one to be easily forgotten, and yet eyes, hair, expression, combined to remind him of some one whom he had seen but could not bring definitely to mind. There were no names on the locket, no marks of identification of any kind, yet realizing the sacredness of it,

Keith slipped the fragile gold chain about his neck, and securely hid the trinket beneath his shirt.

It was noon by this time, the sun high overhead, and his horse, with dangling rein, still nibbling daintily at the short grass. There was no reason for his lingering longer. He swept his gaze the length and breadth of the desolate valley, and across the river over the sand hills. All alike appeared deserted, not a moving thing being visible between the bluffs and the stream. Still he had the unpleasant feeling of being watched, and it made him restless and eager to be away. The earlier gust of anger, the spirit of revenge, had left him, but it had merely changed into a dogged resolution to discover the perpetrators of this outrage and bring them to justice for the crime. The face in the locket seemed to ask it of him, and his nature urged response. But he could hope to accomplish nothing more here, and the plainsman swung himself into the saddle. He turned his horse's head eastward, and rode away. From the deeply rutted trail he looked back to where the fire still smoked in the midst of that desolate silence.

# CHAPTER III

## AN ARREST

THE Santa Fé trail was far too exposed to be safely travelled alone and in broad daylight, but Keith considered it better to put sufficient space between himself and those whom he felt confident were still watching his movements from across the river. How much they might already suspicion his discoveries he possessed no means of knowing, yet, conscious of their own guilt, they might easily feel safer if he were also put out of the way. He had no anticipation of open attack, but must guard against treachery. As he rode, his eyes never left those far-away sand dunes, although he perceived no movement, no black dot even which he could conceive to be a possible enemy. Now that he possessed ample time for thought, the situation became more puzzling. This tragedy which he had accidentally stumbled upon must have had a cause other than blind chance. It was the culmination of a plot, with some reason behind more important than ordinary robbery. Apparently the wagons contained nothing of value, merely the clothing, provisions, and ordinary utensils

28

of an emigrant party. Nor had the victims' pockets been carefully searched. Only the mules had been taken by the raiders, and they would be small booty for such a crime.

The trail, continually skirting the high bluff and bearing farther away from the river, turned sharply into a narrow ravine. There was a considerable break in the rocky barrier here, leading back for perhaps a hundred yards, and the plainsman turned his horse that way, dismounting when out of sight among the bowlders. He could rest here until night with little danger of discovery. He lay down on the rocks, pillowing his head on the saddle, but his brain was too active to permit sleeping. Finally he drew the letters from out his pocket, and began examining them. They yielded very little information, those taken from the older man having no envelopes to show to whom they had been addressed. The single document found in the pocket of the other was a memorandum of account at the Pioneer Store at Topeka, charged to John Sibley, and marked paid. This then must have been the younger man's name, as the letters to the other began occasionally " Dear Will." They were missives such as a wife might write to a husband long absent, yet upon a mission of deep interest to both. Keith could not fully determine what this mission might be, as the persons evidently understood each other so thoroughly that mere allusion took the place of detail. Twice the name Phyllis was mentioned, and once a " Fred " was also referred to, but in neither instance clearly enough to reveal the relationship, although the latter appeared to be pleaded for. Certain references caused the belief that these letters had been mailed from some small Missouri town, but no name was mentioned. They were invariably signed " Mary." The only other paper Keith discovered was a brief itinerary of the Santa Fé trail extending as far west as the Raton Mountains, giving the usual camping spots and places where water was accessible. He slipped the papers back into his pocket with a distinct feeling of disappointment, and lay back staring up at the little strip of blue sky. The silence was profound, even his horse standing motionless, and finally he fell asleep.

The sun had disappeared, and even the gray of twilight was fading out of the sky, when Keith returned again to consciousness, aroused by his horse rolling on the soft turf. He awoke thoroughly refreshed, and eager to get away on his long night's ride. A cold lunch, hastily eaten, for a fire would have been dangerous, and he saddled up and was off, trotting out of the narrow ravine and into the broad trail, which could be followed without difficulty under the dull gleam of the stars. Horse and rider were soon at their best, the animal swinging unurged into the long, easy lope of prairie travel, the fresh air fanning the man's face as he leaned forward. Once they halted to drink from a narrow stream, and then pushed on, hour after hour, through the deserted night. Keith had little fear of Indian raiders in that darkness, and every stride of his horse brought him closer to the settlements and further removed from danger. Yet eyes and ears were alert to every shadow and sound. Once, it must have been after midnight, he drew his pony sharply back into a rock shadow at the noise of something approaching from the east. The stage to Santa Fé rattled past, the four mules trotting swiftly, a squad of troopers riding hard behind. It was merely a lumping shadow sweeping swiftly past; he could perceive the dim outlines of driver and guard, the soldiers swaying in their saddles, heard the pounding of hoofs, the creak of axles, and then the apparition disappeared into the black void. He had not called out — what was the use? Those people would never pause to hunt down prairie outlaws, and their guard was sufficient to prevent attack. They acknowledged but one duty — to get the mail through on time.

The dust of their passing still in the air, Keith rode on, the noise dying away in his rear. As the hours passed, his horse wearied and had to be spurred into the swifter stride, but the man seemed tireless. The sun was an hour high when they climbed the long hill, and loped into Carson City. The cantonment was to the right, but Keith, having no report to make, rode directly ahead down the one long street to a livery corral, leaving his horse there, and sought the nearest restaurant.

Exhausted by a night of high play and deep drinking the border town was sleeping off its debauch, saloons and gambling dens silent, the streets almost deserted. To Keith, whose former acquaintance with the place had been entirely after nightfall, the view of it now was almost a shock — the miserable shacks, the gaudy saloon fronts, the littered streets, the dingy, unpainted hotel, the dirty flap of canvas, the unoccupied road, the dull prairie sweeping away to the horizon, all composed a hideous picture beneath the sun glare. He could scarcely find a man to attend his horse, and at the restaurant a drowsy Chinaman had to be shaken awake, and frightened into serving him. He sat down to the miserable meal oppressed with disgust — never before had his life seemed so mean, useless, utterly without excuse.

He possessed the appetite of the open, of the normal man in perfect physical health, and he ate heartily, his eyes wandering out of the open window down the long, dismal street. A drunken man lay in front of the " Red Light " Saloon sleeping undisturbed; two cur dogs were snarling at each other just beyond over a bone; a movers' wagon was slowly coming in across the open through a cloud of yellow dust. That was all within the radius of vision. For the first time in years the East called him — the old life of cleanliness and respectability. He swore to himself as he tossed the Chinaman pay for his breakfast, and strode out onto the steps. Two men were coming up the street together from the opposite direction — one lean, dark-skinned, with black goatee, the other heavily set with closely trimmed gray beard. Keith knew the latter, and waited, leaning against the door, one hand on his hip.

"Hullo, Bob," he said genially; "they must have routed you out pretty early to-day."

"They shore did, Jack," was the response. He came up the steps somewhat heavily, his companion stopping below. "The boys raise hell all night, an' then come ter me ter straighten it out in the mawnin'. When did ye git in?"

"An hour ago; had to wake the 'chink' up to get any chuck. Town looks dead."

"Tain't over lively at this time o' day," permitting his blue eyes to wander up the silent street, but instantly

3

bringing them back to Keith's face, " but I reckon it 'll wake up later on."

He stood squarely on both feet, and one hand rested on the butt of a revolver. Keith noticed this, wondering vaguely.

" I reckon yer know, Jack, as how I ginerally git what I goes after," said the slow, drawling voice, " an' that I draw 'bout as quick as any o' the boys. They tell me yo 're a gun-fighter, but it won't do ye no good ter make a play yere, fer one o' us is sure to git yer — do yer sabe? "

" Get me? " Keith's voice and face expressed astonishment, but not a muscle of his body moved. " What do you mean, Bob — are you fellows after me? "

" Sure thing; got the warrant here," and he tapped the breast of his shirt with his left hand.

The color mounted into the cheeks of the other, his lips grew set and white, and his gray eyes darkened.

" Let it all out, Marshal," he said sternly, " you 've got me roped and tied. Now what 's the charge? "

Neither man moved, but the one below swung about so as to face them, one hand thrust out of sight beneath the tail of his long coat.

" Make him throw up his hands, Bob," he said sharply.

" Oh, I reckon thar ain't goin' ter be no trouble,"

returned the marshal genially, yet with no relaxation of attention. " Keith knows me, an' expects a fair deal. Still, maybe I better ask yer to unhitch yer belt, Jack."

A moment Keith seemed to hesitate, plainly puzzled by the situation and endeavoring to see some way of escape; then his lips smiled, and he silently unhooked the belt, handing it over.

" Sure, I know you 're square, Hicks," he said, coolly. " And now I 've unlimbered, kindly inform me what this is all about."

" I reckon yer don't know."

" No more than an unborn babe. I have been here but an hour."

" That 's it: if yer had been longer thar would n't be no trouble. Yo 're wanted for killin' a couple o' men out at Cimmaron Crossin' early yesterday mornin'."

Keith stared at him too completely astounded for the instant to even speak. Then he gasped.

" For God's sake, Hicks, do you believe that? "

" I 'm damned if I know," returned the marshal, doubtfully. " Don't seem like ye 'd do it, but the evidence is straight 'nough, an' thar ain't nothin' fer me ter do but take ye in. I ain't no jedge an' jury."

" No, but you ought to have ordinary sense, an' you 've known me for three years."

" Sure I have, Jack, but if yer 've gone wrong, you won't be the first good man I 've seen do it. Anyhow, the evidence is dead agin you, an' I 'd arrest my own grand-dad if they give me a warrant agin him."

" What evidence is there? "

" Five men swear they saw ye haulin' the bodies about, and lootin' the pockets."

Then Keith understood, his heart beating rapidly, his teeth clenched to keep back an outburst of passion. So that was their game, was it? — some act of his had awakened the cowardly suspicions of those watching him across the river. They were afraid that he knew them as white men. And they had found a way to safely muzzle him. They must have ridden hard over those sand dunes to have reached Carson City and sworn out this warrant. It was a good trick, likely enough to hang him, if the fellows only stuck to their story. All this flashed through his brain, yet somehow he could not clearly comprehend the full meaning, his mind confused and dazed by this sudden realization of danger. His eyes wandered from the steady gaze of the marshal, who had half drawn his gun fearing resistance, to the man at the bottom of the steps. Suddenly it dawned upon him where he had seen that dark-skinned face, with the black goatee, before — at the

faro table of the " Red Light." He gripped his hands
together, instantly connecting that sneering, sinister face
with the plot.

" Who swore out that warrant? "

" I did, if you need to know," a sarcastic smile revealing a gleam of white teeth, " on the affidavit of
others, friends of mine."

" Who are you? "

" I 'm mostly called ' Black Bart.' "

That was it; he had the name now —" Black Bart."
He straightened up so quickly, his eyes blazing, that
the marshal jerked his gun clear.

" See here, Jack," shortly, " are yer goin' to raise
a row, or come along quiet? "

As though the words had aroused him from a bad
dream, Keith turned to front the stern, bearded face.

" There 'll be no row, Bob," he said, quietly. " I 'll
go with you."

# CHAPTER IV

## AN OLD ACQUAINTANCE

THE Carson City lock-up was an improvised affair,
although a decidedly popular resort. It was originally a two-room cabin with gable to the street, the
front apartment at one time a low groggery, the keeper
sleeping in the rear room. Whether sudden death, or
financial reverses, had been the cause, the community
had in some manner become possessed of the property,
and had at once dedicated it to the commonweal. For
the purpose thus selected it was rather well adapted, being strongly built, easily guarded, and on the outskirts of
the town. With iron grating over the windows, the
back door heavily spiked, and the front secured by
iron bars, any prisoner once locked within could
probably be found when wanted. On the occasion of
Keith's arrival, the portion abutting upon the street
was occupied by a rather miscellaneous assembly —
the drunk and disorderly element conspicuous — who
were awaiting their several calls to appear before a
local justice and make answer for various misdeeds.
Some were pacing the floor, others sat moodily on

benches ranged against the wall, while a few were still peacefully slumbering upon the floor. It was a frowsy, disreputable crowd, evincing but mild curiosity at the arrival of a new prisoner. Keith had barely time to glance about, recognizing no familiarity of face amid the mass peering at him, as he was hustled briskly forward and thrust into the rear room, the heavy door closing behind him with the snap of a spring lock.

He was alone, with only the faintest murmur of voices coming to him through the thick partition. It was a room some twelve feet square, open to the roof, with bare walls, and containing no furniture except a rude bench. Still dazed by the suddenness of his arrest, he sank down upon the seat, leaned his head on his hands, and endeavored to think. It was difficult to get the facts marshalled into any order or to comprehend clearly the situation, yet little by little his brain grasped the main details, and he awoke to a full realization of his condition, of the forces he must war against. The actual murderers of those two men on the trail had had their suspicions aroused by his actions; they believed he guessed something of their foul deed, and had determined to clear themselves by charging the crime directly against him. It was a shrewd trick, and if they only stuck to their story, ought to succeed. He had no evidence, other than his own word, and the marshal

had already taken from his pockets the papers belonging to the slain man. He had not found the locket
hidden under his shirt, yet a more thorough search
would doubtless reveal that also.

Even should the case come to trial, how would it be
possible for him to establish innocence, and — *would
it ever come to trial?* Keith knew the character of
the frontier, and of Carson City. The inclination of
its citizens in such cases was to act first, and reflect
later. The law had but slender hold, being respected
only when backed by the strong hand, and primitive
instincts were always in the ascendency, requiring
merely a leader to break forth into open violence.
And in this case would there be any lack of leadership?
Like a flash his mind reverted to " Black Bart." There
was the man capable of inciting a mob. If, for some
unknown reason, he had sufficient interest to swear
out the warrant and assist in the arrest, he would
have equal cause to serve those fellows behind him in
other ways. Naturally, they would dread a trial, with
its possibility of exposure, and eagerly grasp any opportunity for wiping the slate clean. Their real se-
curity from discovery undoubtedly lay in his death,
and with the " Red Light " crowd behind them they
would experience no trouble in getting a following desperate enough for any purpose.

The longer Keith thought the less he doubted the result. It was not then a problem of defence, but of escape, for he believed now that no opportunity to defend himself would ever be allowed. The arrest was merely part of the plot intended to leave him helpless in the hands of the mob. In this Hicks was in no way blamable — he had merely performed his sworn duty, and would still die, if need be, in defence of his prisoner. He was no tool, but only an instrument they had found means of using.

Keith was essentially a man of action, a fighter by instinct, and so long accustomed to danger that the excitement of it merely put new fire into his veins. Now that he understood exactly what threatened, all numbing feeling of hesitancy and doubt vanished, and he became instantly alive. He would not lie there in that hole waiting for the formation of a mob; nor would he trust in the ability of the marshal to defend him.

He had some friends without — not many, for he was but an occasional visitor at Carson — who would rally to Hicks's assistance, but there would not be enough on the side of law and order to overcome the " Red Light " outfit, if once they scented blood. If he was to be saved from their clutches, he must save himself; if his innocence was ever established it would be by his own exertions — and he could accomplish this only out yonder, free under the arch of sky.

He lifted his head, every nerve tingling with desperate determination. The low growl of voices was audible through the partition, but there was no other sound. Carson City was still resting, and there would be no crowd nor excitement until much later. Not until nightfall would any attack be attempted; he had six or eight hours yet in which to perfect his plans. He ran his eyes about the room searching for some spot of weakness. It was dark back of the bench, and he turned in that direction. Leaning over, he looked down on the figure of a man curled up, sound asleep on the floor. The fellow's limbs twitched as if in a dream, otherwise he might have deemed him dead, as his face was buried in his arms. A moment Keith hesitated; then he reached down and shook the sleeper, until he aroused sufficiently to look up. It was the face of a coal-black negro. An instant the fellow stared at the man towering over him, his thick lips parted, his eyes full of sudden terror. Then he sat up, with hands held before him as though warding off a blow.

"Fo' de Lawd's sake," he managed to articulate finally, "am dis sho' yo', Massa Jack?"

Keith, to whom all colored people were much alike, laughed at the expression on the negro's face.

"I reckon yer guessed the name, all right, boy. Were you the cook of the Diamond L?"

"No, sah, I nebber cooked no di'onds. I 'se ol' Neb, sah."

"What?"

"Yes, sah, I 'se de boy dat libbed wid ol' Missus Caton durin' de wah. I ain't seen yo', Massa Jack, sence de day we buried yo' daddy, ol' Massa Keith. But I knowed yo' de berry minute I woke up. Sho', yo' 'members Neb, sah?"

It came to Keith now in sudden rush of memory — the drizzling rain in the little cemetery, the few neighbors standing about, a narrow fringe of slaves back of them, the lowering of the coffin, and the hollow sound of earth falling on the box; and Neb, his Aunt Caton's house servant, a black imp of good humor, who begged so hard to be taken back with him to the war. Why, the boy had held his stirrup the next morning when he rode away. The sudden rush of recollection seemed to bridge the years, and that black face became familiar, a memory of home.

"Of course, I remember, Neb," he exclaimed, eagerly, "but that's all years ago and I never expected to see you again. What brought you West and got you into this hole?"

The negro hitched up onto the bench, the whites of

his eyes conspicuous as he stared uneasily about — he had a short, squatty figure, with excessively broad shoulders, and a face of intense good humor.

"I reck'n dat am consider'ble ob a story, Massa Jack, de circumlocution ob which would take a heap ob time tellin'," he began soberly. "But it happened 'bout dis away. When de Yankees come snoopin' long de East Sho'— I reck'n maybe it des a yeah after dat time when we done buried de ol' Co'nel — dey burned Missus Caton's house clah to de groun'; de ol' Missus was in Richmond den, an' de few niggers left jest natchally took to de woods. I went into Richmond huntin' de ol' Missus, but, Lawd, Massa Jack, I nebber foun' nuthin' ob her in dat crowd. Den an' officer man done got me, an' put me diggin' in de trenches. Ef dat 's what wah am, I sho' don' want no mo' wah. Den after dat I jest natchally drifted. I reckon I libbed 'bout eberywhar yo' ebber heard ob, fo' dar want no use ob me goin' back to de East Sho'. Somebody said dat de West am de right place fo' a nigger, an' so I done headed west."

He dropped his face in his black hands, and was silent for some minutes, but Keith said nothing, and finally the thick voice continued:

"I tell yo', Massa Jack, it was mighty lonely fo' Neb dem days. I did n't know whar any ob yo'

all was, an' it wan't no fun fo' dis nigger bein' free
dat away.  I got out ter Independence, Missouri, an' was
roustaboutin' on de ribber, when a coupple ob men come
along what wanted a cook to trabbel wid 'em.  I took
de job, an' dat 's what fetched me here ter Carson City."

" But what caused your arrest? "

" A conjunction ob circumstances, Massa Jack; yes,
sah, a conjunction ob circumstances.  I got playin'
pokah ober in dat ' Red Light,' an' I was doin' fine.
I reckon I 'd cleaned up mo'n a hundred dollars when
I got sleepy, an' started fo' camp.  I 'd most got dar
w'en a bunch ob low white trash jumped me.  It made
me mad, it did fo' a fact, an' I reckon I carved some ob
'em up befo' I got away.  Ennyhow, de marshal come
down, took me out ob de tent, an' fetched me here, an'
I ben here ebber sence.  I wan't goin' ter let no low
down white trash git all dat money."

" What became of the men you were working for? "

" I reckon dey went on, sah.  Dey had 'portent
business, an' would n't likely wait 'roun' here jest ter
help a nigger.  Ain't ennybody ben here ter see me, no-
how, an' I 'spects I 'se eradicated from dey mem'ry —
I 'spects I is."

# CHAPTER V

## THE ONE WAY

KEITH said nothing for some moments, staring up at the light stealing in through the window grating, his mind once again active. The eyes of the black man had the patient look of a dog as they watched; evidently he had cast aside all responsibility, now that this other had come. Finally Keith spoke slowly:

"We are in much the same position, Neb, and the fate of one is liable to be the fate of both. This is my story "— and briefly as possible, he ran over the circumstances which had brought him there, putting the situation clear enough for the negro's understanding, without wasting any time upon detail. Neb followed his recital with bulging eyes, and an occasional exclamation. At the end he burst forth:

"Yo' say dar was two ob dem white men murdered — one an ol' man wid a gray beard, an' de odder 'bout thirty? Am dat it, Massa Jack, an' dey had fo' span ob mules, an' a runnin' hoss?"

"Yes."

"An' how far out was it?"

46

" About sixty miles."

" Oh, de good Lawd! " and the negro threw up his hands dramatically. " Dat sutt'nly am my outfit! Dat am Massa Waite an' John Sibley."

" You mean the same men with whom you came here from Independence? "

Neb nodded, overcome by the discovery.

" But what caused them to run such a risk? " Keith insisted. " Did n't they know the Indians were on the war path? "

" Sho'; I heard 'em talkin' 'bout dat, but Massa Waite was jest boun' foh to git movin'. He did n't 'pear to be 'fraid ob no Injuns; reck'ned dey 'd nebber stop him, dat he knowed ebbery chief on de plains. I reck'n dat he did, too."

" But what was he so anxious to get away for? "

" I dunno, Massa, I done heerd 'em talk some 'bout dey plans, an' 'bout some gal dey wanted ter fin', but I did n't git no right sense to it. De Gin'ral, he was a mighty still man."

" The General? Whom do you mean? Not Waite? "

" John Sibley done called him dat."

Then Keith remembered — just a dim, misty thread at first, changing slowly into a clear recollection. He was riding with despatches from Longstreet to Stonewall Jackson, and had been shot through the side. The first of Jackson's troops he reached was a brigade of North Carolinians, commanded by General Waite — General Willis Waite. He had fallen from his horse at the outposts, was brought helpless to the General's tent, and another sent on with the papers. And Mrs. Waite had dressed and bandaged his wound. That was where he had seen that woman's face before, with its haunting familiarity. He drew the locket from beneath his shirt, and gazed at the countenance revealed, with new intelligence. There could be no doubt — it was the face of her who had cared for him so tenderly in that tent at Manassas before the fever came and he had lost consciousness. And that, then, was Willis Waite lying in that shallow grave near the Cimmaron Crossing, and for whose death he had been arrested. 'T was a strange world, and a small one. What a miserable ending to a life like his — a division commander of the Army of Northern Virginia, a Lieutenant-Governor of his State. What strange combination of circumstances could ever have brought such a man to this place, and sent him forth across those Indian-scouted plains? Surely nothing ordinary. And why should those border desperadoes have followed, through sixty miles of desolation, to strike him down? It was not robbery, at least

in the ordinary sense. What then? And how was
" Black Bart " involved? Why should he be sufficiently interested to swear out a warrant, and then
assist in his arrest? There must be something to all
this not apparent upon the surface — some object, some
purpose shrouded in mystery. No mere quarrel, no
ordinary feud, no accident of meeting, no theory of
commonplace robbery, would account for the deed, or
for the desperate efforts now being made to conceal it.

Some way, these questions, thus surging upon him,
became a call to live, to fight, to unravel their mystery.
The memory of that sweet-faced woman who had bent
above him when the fever began its mastery, appealed
to him now with the opportunity of service. He might
be able to clear this, bring to her the truth, save her
from despair, and hand over to justice the murderers
of her husband. It was up to him alone to accomplish this — no one else knew what he knew, suspected what he suspected. And there was but one way
— through escape. To remain there in weak surrender
to fate could have but one ending, and that swift and
sudden. He had no doubt as to " Black Bart's " purpose, or of his ability to use the " Red Light " outfit as
desired. The whole plan was clearly evident, and
there would be no delay in execution — all they were

4

waiting for was night, and a lax guard. He glanced about at the walls of the room, his eyes grown hard, his teeth clenched.

" Neb," he said shortly, " I guess that was your outfit all right, but they were not killed by Indians. They were run down by a gang from this town — the same fellows who have put you and me in here. I don't know what they were after — that 's to be found out later,— but the fight you put up at the camp spoiled their game for once, and led to your arrest. They failed to get what was wanted in Carson, and so they trailed the party to the Cimmaron Crossing. Then I got on their track, and fearing the result, they 've landed me also. Now they 'll get rid of us both as best they can. These fellows won't want any trial — that would be liable to give the whole trick away — but they have got to put us where we won't talk. There is an easy way to do this, and that is by a lynching bee. Do you get my drift, Neb ? "

The whites of the negro's eyes were very much in evidence, his hands gripping at the bench on which he sat.

" Fo' de Lawd, yes, Massa Jack, I sho' does. I corroborates de whole thing."

" Then you are willing to take a chance with me ? "

" Willin' ! Why, Massa Jack, I 'se overjoyed; I

ain't gwine leave yer no mo'. I 'se sho' gwine ter be yo' nigger. What yo' gwine ter do?"

Keith ran his eyes over the walls, carefully noting every peculiarity.

"We 'll remain here quietly just as long as it is daylight, Neb," he replied finally, " but we 'll try every board and every log to discover some way out. Just the moment it grows dark enough to slip away without being seen we 've got to hit the prairie. Once south of the Arkansas we 're safe, but not until then. Have you made any effort to get out?"

The negro came over to him, and bent down.

"I was layin' on a board what I 'd worked loose at one end," he whispered hoarsely, " back ob de bench, but I could n't jerk it out wid'out somethin' ter pry it up wid."

"Where is it?"

"Right yere, Massa Jack."

It was a heavy twelve-inch plank, part of the flooring, and the second from the side-wall. Keith managed to get a grip next to the black fingers, and the two pressed it up far enough for the white man to run one arm through the opening up to his shoulder and grope about below.

"There 's a two-foot space there," he reported, as they let the board settle silently down into position.

"The back part of this building must be set up on piles. I reckon we could pry that plank up with the bench, Neb, but it's liable to make considerable racket. Let's hunt about first for some other weak spot."

They crept across the floor, testing each separate board, but without discovering a place where they could exert a leverage. The thick planks were tightly spiked down. Nor did the walls offer any better encouragement. Keith lifted himself to the grated window, getting a glimpse of the world without, but finding the iron immovable, the screws solidly imbedded in the outside wood. He dropped to the floor, feeling baffled and discouraged.

"It will have to be the plank back of the bench, Neb," he announced briefly, wiping the perspiration from his face. "Get down there, and work it as loose as you can without making any noise, while I keep my ear to the door and listen for any interruption."

They took turns at this labor, discovering a loose nail which gave an opening purchase at the crack, thus enabling the insertion of a small wooden block, and insuring space for a good finger grip when the right time came. A sleepy Mexican brought in their dinner, and set it down on the bench without a word, but on his return with supper, the marshal accompanied him, and remained while they ate, talking to Keith, and staring about the room. Fortunately, the single window was to the west, and the last rays of the sun struck the opposite wall, leaving the space behind the bench in deep shadow. Whatever might be the plans of " Black Bart " and his cronies, Keith was soon convinced they were unknown to Hicks, who had evidently been deceived into thinking that this last arrest had created no excitement.

" That's why we picked yer up so early," he explained, genially. " Bart said if we got to yer afore the boys woke up they'd never hear nuthin' 'bout it, an' so thar would n't be no row. He did n't even think thar 'd be enny need o' keepin' a special guard ter-night, but I reckon I won't take no such chance as that, an' I 'll have a couple o' deputies prowlin' 'round fer luck. When Carson does wake up, she 's hell."

He left them tobacco and pipes, and went away evidently convinced that he had performed his full duty. The two prisoners, puffing smoke-rings into the air, heard the heavy clang of the iron bar falling into place across the door, and sat looking into one another's faces through the deepening twilight. In the mind of both black and white reposed the same thought. The negro was first to break the silence.

" 'Pears ter me, Massa Jack, like dis yere Bart pusson am mighty anxious ter hab no suspicions raised."

" Anybody but Hicks would see that," acknowledged the other, the rings of smoke circling his head, " but he has n't any brains. It was pure nerve that got him the job. Well, this is one time that ' Bart pusson ' is going to find an empty coop. We 'll get out, Neb, just as soon as it gets dark enough. Hicks is n't likely to put on his extra guard for an hour yet, and the ' Red Light ' bunch won't be fit for business much before midnight. By that time we 'll be in the sand hills, heading south, able to give them a run for their money — we 'll have horses, too, if we can find them."

The negro's eyes shone white.

" Fo' de Lawd's sake, Massa," he protested, " dat 'd sho' be a hangin' job if ebber dey cotched us."

Keith laughed, knocking out the ashes from his pipe.

" With an hour's start that will be the least of my troubles," he said, quietly.

# CHAPTER VI

### THE ESCAPE

IT was dark enough for their purpose in half an hour, the only gleam of remaining color being the red glow of the negro's pipe, even the openings in the iron grating being blotted from sight. Keith, staring in that direction, failed to perceive any distant glimmer of star, and decided the night must be cloudy, and that time for action had come. Guided by Neb's pipe bowl, he touched the boy on the shoulder.

"Knock out your ashes, and shuffle about lively with your feet, while I pry up the board."

In spite of his slenderness, Keith possessed unusual strength, yet no exertion on his part served to start the loosened plank sufficiently for their purpose. Ripping a strip from the bench he managed to pry the hole somewhat larger, arranging the bench itself so as to afford the necessary leverage, but even then his entire weight failed to either start the spikes, or crack the plank. Some altercation began in the other room, the sound of angry voices and shuffling feet being plainly audible. It was clear to Keith that they must take the chance of a noise, and no better time than this could be chosen.

"Here, Neb, take hold with me, and bear down — put your whole weight on it, boy."

The two flung themselves upon the end of the bench, leaping up and down so as to add weight to power. Something had to give, either the stout wood of their improvised lever or else the holding of the plank. For an instant it seemed likely to be the former; then, with a shrill screech, the long spikes yielded and the board suddenly gave. With shoulders inserted beneath, the two men heaved it still higher, ramming the bench below so as to leave the opening clear. This was now sufficiently ample for the passage of a man's body, and Keith, lowering himself, discovered the earth to be fully four feet below. The negro instantly joined him, and they began creeping about in the darkness, seeking some way out. A rudely laid foundation of limestone alone obstructed their path to the open air. This had been laid in mortar, but of inferior quality, so that little difficulty was experienced in detaching sufficient to obtain hand hold. Working silently, not knowing what watchers might be already stationed without, they succeeded in loosening enough of the rock to allow them to crawl through, lying breathless in the open. Accustomed as they were to the darkness, they could yet see little. They were upon the opposite side from the town, with no gleam of lights visible, prairie and sky blending together into spectral dimness, with no sound audible but the continued quarrel in the front room of the jail. Keith crept along to the end of the building from where he could perceive the lights of the town twinkling dimly through the intense blackness. Evidently the regular evening saturnalia had not yet begun, although there was already semblance of life about the numerous saloons, and an occasional shout punctuated the stillness. A dog howled in the distance, and the pounding of swift hoofs along the trail told of fresh arrivals. An hour later and the single street of Carson City would be alive with humanity, eager for any excitement, ready for any wild orgy, if only once turned loose. That it would be turned loose, and also directed, the man lying on his face in the grass felt fully assured. He smiled grimly, wishing he might behold " Black Bart's " face when he should discover the flight of his intended victims. But there was no time to lose; every moment gained, added to their chance of safety.

" Are those horses tied there by the blacksmith's shop? " he asked, pointing.

The negro stared in the direction indicated, confused by the shadows thrown by the dim lights.

" I reck'n dey am, Massa Jack; I done make out fo'."

" Then two of them must belong to us; come on, boy."

He ran forward, crouching behind every chance cover, and keeping well back behind the line of shacks. A slight depression in the prairie helped conceal their movements, and neither spoke until they were crouching together beside the wall of the shop.  Then Neb, teeth chattering, managed to blurt forth:

" Fo' de Lawd's sake, yer don't actually mean ter steal dem hosses? "

Keith glanced about at the other's dim, black shadow.

" Sure not; just borrow 'em."

" But dat 's a hangin' job in dis yere country, Massa Jack."

" Sure it is if they catch us.  But we 'd be strung up anyway, and we can't be hung twice.  Besides there is a chance for us with the ponies, and none at all without.  An hour's start in the saddle, Neb, and this bunch back here will never even find our trail; I pledge you that.  Come, boy, stay close with me."

It was the quiet, confident voice of assured command, of one satisfied with his plans, and the obedient negro, breathing hard, never dreamed of opposition; all instincts of slavery held him to the dominion of this white master. Keith leaned forward, staring at the string of deserted ponies tied to the rail. Success depended on his choice, and he could judge very little in that darkness. Men were straggling in along the street to their right, on foot and horseback, and the saloon on the corner was being well patronized. A glow of light streamed forth from its windows, and there was the sound of many voices. But this narrow alley was deserted, and black. The fugitive stepped boldly forward, afraid that otherwise he might startle the ponies and thus create an alarm. Guided by a horseman's instinct he swiftly ran his hands over the animals, and made quick selection.

"Here, Neb, take this fellow; lead him quietly down the bank," and he thrust the loosened rein into the black's hand.

An instant later he had chosen his own mount, and was silently moving in the same direction, although the night there was so black that the obedient negro had already entirely vanished. The slope of the land not only helped cover their movements, but also rendered it easy for them to find one another. Fully a hundred yards westward they met, where a gully led directly down toward the river. There was no longer need for remaining on foot, as they were a sufficient distance away from the little town to feel no fear of being discovered, unless by some drunken straggler. At Keith's command the negro climbed into his saddle. Both ponies were restive, but not vicious, and after a plunge or two, to test their new masters, came easily under control. Keith led the way, moving straight down the gully, which gradually deepened, burying them in its black heart, until it finally debouched onto the river sands. The riotous noises of the drunken town died slowly away behind, the night silent and dark. The two riders could scarcely distinguish one another as they drew rein at the edge of the water. To the southward there gleamed a cluster of lights, marking the position of the camp of regulars. Keith drove his horse deeper into the stream, and headed northward, the negro following like a shadow.

There was a ford directly opposite the cantonment, and another, more dangerous, and known to only a few, three miles farther up stream. Keeping well within the water's edge, so as to thus completely obscure their trail, yet not daring to venture deep for fear of striking quicksand, the plainsman sent his pony struggling forward, until the dim outline of the bank at his right rendered him confident that they had attained the proper point for crossing. He had been that way only once before, and realized the danger of attempting passage in such darkness, but urgent need drove him forward.

" Follow me just as close as you can, boy," he said sternly, " and keep both your feet out of the stirrups. If your horse goes down hang to his tail, and let him swim out."

There was little enough to guide by, merely a single faint star peering out from a rift of the clouds, but Keith's remembrance was that the ford led straight out to the centre of the stream, and then veered slightly toward the right. He knew the sand ridge was only used by horsemen, not being wide enough for the safe passage of wagons, but the depth of the water on either side was entirely problematical. He was taking a big chance, yet dare not wait for daylight. Summoning all his nerve and alertness, he urged his horse slowly forward, the intelligent animal seemingly comprehending the situation, and feeling carefully for footing. The actions of the animal gave the rider greater confidence, and he loosened his grip on the rein, leaving the pony's instinct to control. The latter fairly crept forward, testing the sand before resting any weight upon the hoof, the negro's mount following closely. The water was unusually high, and as they advanced it bore down against them in considerable volume; then, as they veered to the right, they were compelled to push directly against its weight in struggling toward shore. The men could see nothing but this solid sheet of water rushing down toward them from out the black void, and then vanishing below. Once Keith's horse half fell, plunging nose under, yet gaining foothold again before the rider had deserted his saddle. A dim blackness ahead already revealed the nearness of the southern bank, when Neb's pony went down suddenly, swept fairly off its legs by some fierce eddy in the stream. Keith heard the negro's guttural cry, and caught a glimpse of him as the two were sent whirling down. The coiled rope of the lariat, grasped in his right hand, was hurled forth like a shot, but came back empty. Not another sound reached him; his own horse went steadily on, feeling his way, until he was nose against the bank, with water merely rippling about his ankles. Keith driving feet again into the stirrups headed him down stream, wading close in toward the shore, leaning forward over the pommel striving to see through the gloom.

He had no doubt about Neb's pony making land, unless struck by some driftwood, or borne to the centre of the stream by the shifting force of the current. But if Neb had failed to retain his grip he might have been sucked under by the surge of waters. A hundred yards below he found them, dripping and weak from the struggle, yet otherwise unhurt. There were no words spoken, but black and white hands clasped silently, and then Neb crept back into the saddle, shivering in his wet clothes as the cool night wind swept against him. Keeping close in toward shore, yet far enough out so that the water would hide their trail, the fugitives toiled steadily up stream, guided only by the black outline of the low bank upon their left.

# CHAPTER VII

## IN THE SAND DESERT

SUDDENLY Keith halted, bringing his pony's head sharply about, so that the two faced one another. The wind was rising, hurling clouds of sand into their eyes, and the plainsman held one hand before his face.

"There's no need of keeping up a water trail any longer," he said quietly. "By all the signs we're in for a sand storm by daylight, and that will cover our tracks so the devil himself couldn't follow them. Got a water bag on your saddle?"

"I reck'n dis am one, sah."

Keith felt of the object Neb held forth.

"Yes, and a big one, too; fill it and strap it on tight; we've got a long, dry ride ahead."

"Whar' yo' propose goin', Massa Jack?"

"To the 'Bar X' on the Canadian. I've worked with that outfit. They'll give us whatever we need, and ask no questions; I don't know of anything in between. It's going to be a hard ride, boy, and mighty little to eat except what I saved from supper."

64

" How far am it to dis yere ' Bar X '? "

" A hundred and fifty miles as the crow flies, and sand all the way, except for the valley of Salt Fork. Come on now, and keep close, for it's easy to get lost in these sand hills."

Keith had ridden that hundred and fifty miles of sandy desolation before, but had never been called upon to make such a journey as this proved to be. He knew there was little to fear from human enemies, for they were riding far enough east of the Santa Fé trail to be out of the path of raiding parties, while this desert country was shunned by Indian hunters. It consisted of sand hill after sand hill, a drear waterless waste where nothing grew, and amid the dread sameness of which a traveller could only find passage by the guidance of stars at night or the blazing sun by day. To the eye mile after mile appeared exactly alike, with nothing whatever to distinguish either distance or direction — the same drifting ridges of sand stretching forth in every direction, no summit higher than another, no semblance of green shrubbery, or silver sheen of running water anywhere to break the dull monotony — a vast sandy plain, devoid of life, extending to the horizon, overhung by a barren sky.

They had covered ten miles of it by daybreak, their ponies travelling heavily, fetlock deep, but could ad-

5

vance no further.   With the first tint of rose in the east
the brooding storm burst upon them in wild desert fury,
the fierce wind buffeting them back, lashing their faces
with sharp grit until they were unable to bear the pain.
The flying sand smote them in clouds, driven with the
speed of bullets.   In vain they lay flat, urging their
ponies forward; the beasts, maddened and blinded by
the merciless lashing of the sand, refused to face the
storm.   Keith, all sense of direction long since lost,
rolled wearily from the saddle, burrowed under the
partial shelter of a sand dune, and called upon Neb
to follow him.   With their hands and feet they made
a slight wind-break, dragging the struggling ponies into
its protection, and burrowed themselves there, the
clouds of sand skurrying over them so thick as to
obscure the sky, and rapidly burying them altogether
as though in a grave.  Within an hour they were
compelled to dig themselves out, yet it proved partial escape from the pitiless lashing.   The wind howled
like unloosed demons, and the air grew cold, adding to the sting of the grit, when some sudden eddy
hurled it into their hiding place.   To endeavor further
travel would mean certain death, for no one could have
guided a course for a hundred feet through the tem-
pest, which seemed to suck the very breath away.   To
the fugitives came this comfort — if they could not

advance, then no one else could follow, and the storm was completely blotting out their trail.

It was three o'clock before it died sufficiently down for them to venture out. Even then the air remained full of sand, while constantly shifting ridges made travel difficult. Only grim necessity — the suffering of the ponies for water, and their own need for soon reaching the habitation of man and acquiring food — drove them to the early venture. They must attain the valley of the Salt Fork that night, or else perish in the desert — there remained no other choice. Tying neckerchiefs over their horses' eyes, and lying flat themselves, they succeeded in pressing slowly forward, winding in and out among the shifting dunes, with only the wind to guide them. It was an awful trail, the hoofs sinking deep in drifting sand, the struggling ponies becoming so exhausted that their riders finally dismounted, and staggered forward on foot, leading them stumbling blindly after. Once the negro's horse dropped, and had to be lashed to its feet again; once Keith's pony stumbled and fell on him, hurling him face down into the sand, and he would have died there, lacking sufficient strength to lift the dead weight, but for Neb's assistance. As it was he went staggering blindly forward, bruised, and faint from hunger and fatigue. Neither man spoke; they had no breath nor energy left

to waste; every ounce of strength needed to be con-
served for the battle against nature. They were fighting for life; fighting grimly, almost hopelessly, and
alone.

About them night finally closed in, black and starless,
yet fortunately with a gradual dying away of the storm.
For an hour past they had been struggling on, doubting their direction, wondering dully if they were not
lost and merely drifting about in a circle. They had
debated this fiercely once, the ponies standing deject-
edly, tails to the storm, Neb arguing that the wind
still blew from the south, and Keith contending it had
shifted into the westward. The white man won his
way, and they staggered on uncertain, the negro grasping the first pony's tail to keep from being separated
from his companion. Some instinct of the plains must
have guided them, for at last they dragged themselves
out from the desert, the crunching sand under foot
changing into rock, and then to short brittle grass, at
which the ponies nibbled eagerly. The slope led gradually downward, the animals scenting water, and struggling to break away. Swaying in their saddles, the riders let them go, and they never stopped until belly deep
in the stream, their noses buried. The men shivered in
their saddles, until, at last satisfied, the ponies consented
to be forced back up the bank, where they nibbled at

the short tufts of herbage, but in a manner expressive of weariness. Keith flung himself on the ground, every muscle of his body aching, his exposed flesh still smarting from the hail of sand through which they had passed.

He had not the slightest conception as to where they were, except he knew this must be the Salt Fork. Utterly confused by the maze of shifting dunes, through whose intricacies they had somehow found passage, the blackness of the night yielded no clue as to their point of emergence. The volume of water in the stream alone suggested that in their wanderings they must have drifted to the eastward, and come out much lower down than had been originally intended. If so, then they might be almost directly south of Carson City, and in a section with which he was totally unacquainted. One thing was, however, certain — they would be compelled to wait for daylight to ascertain the truth, and decide upon their future movements. There was another barren, sandy stretch of desolation lying between this isolated valley and that of the Canadian, and their horses would never stand to be pushed forward without both rest and food. As to themselves — they had eaten their last crumb long since, but this was not the first time both had known starvation.

Keith arose reluctantly, and removed the saddles

from the animals, hobbling them so they could graze at will.    Neb was propped up beneath an out-cropping of the bank, which partly protected him from the wind, a mere hulk of a shadow.    Keith could not tell whether he slept or not, but made no effort to disturb him.    A moment he stared vacantly about into the black silence, and then lay down, pillowing his head upon a saddle. He found it impossible to sleep, the chill of the wind causing him to turn and twist, in vain search after comfort, while unappeased hunger gnawed incessantly. His eyes ranged about over the dull gloom of the skies until they fell again to the earth level, and then he suddenly sat up, half believing himself in a dream — down the stream, how far away he could not judge, there gleamed a steady, yellowish light.    It was no flicker of a camp fire, yet remained stationary.    Surely no star could be so low and large; nor did he recall any with that peculiarity of color.    If such a miracle was possible in the heart of that sandy desert he would have sworn it was a lamp shining through a window. But he had never heard of any settler on the Salt Fork, and almost laughed at the thought, believing for the instant his brain played him some elfish trick.    Yet that light was no illusion; he rubbed his eyes, only to see it more clearly, convinced now of its reality.    He strode hastily across, and shook Neb into semi-con-

sciousness, dragging him bodily up the bank and pointing down stream.

" Do you see that? " he inquired anxiously. " There,
straight ahead of you? "

The negro stared, shaking with cold, and scarcely
able to stand alone.

" Maybe it am de moon, Massa Jack," he muttered
thickly, " or a goblin's lantern. Lawd, I don't jest like
de looks ob dat ting."

" Well, I do," and Keith laughed uneasily at the
negro's fears. " All I wanted to know was if you saw
what I saw. That's a lamp shining through a window, Neb. What in heaven's name it can be doing
here I am unable to guess, but I'm going to find out.
It means shelter and food, boy, even if we have to fight
for it. Come on, the horses are safe, and we'll discover what is behind that light yonder."

# CHAPTER VIII

## THE WILDERNESS CABIN

THE light was considerably farther away than they had at first supposed, and as they advanced steadily toward it, the nature of the ground rapidly changed, becoming irregular, and littered with low growing shrubs. In the darkness they stumbled over outcroppings of rock, and after a fall or two, were compelled to move forward with extreme caution. But the mysterious yellow glow continually beckoned, and with new hope animating the hearts of both men, they staggered on, nerving themselves to the effort, and following closely along the bank of the stream.

At last they arrived where they could perceive dimly something of the nature of this unexpected desert oasis.

The light shone forth, piercing the night, through the uncurtained window of a log cabin, which would otherwise have been completely concealed from view by a group of low growing cottonwoods. This was all the black, enshrouding night revealed, and even this was merely made apparent by the yellow illumination of the window. The cabin stood upon an island, a strip of sand, partially covered by water, separating it from the north shore on which they stood. There was no sign of life about the hut, other than the burning lamp, but that alone was sufficient evidence of occupancy. In spite of hunger, and urgent need, Keith hesitated, uncertain as to what they might be called upon to face. Who could be living in this out-of-the-way spot, in the heart of this inhospitable desert? It would be no cattle outpost surely, for there was no surrounding grazing land, while surely no professional hunter would choose such a barren spot for headquarters. Either a hermit, anxious to escape all intercourse with humanity, or some outlaw hiding from arrest, would be likely to select so isolated a place in which to live. To them it would be ideal. Away from all trails, where not even widely roving cattlemen would penetrate, in midst of a desert avoided by Indians because of lack of game,— a man might hide here year after year without danger of discovery. Yet such a one would not be likely to welcome their coming, and they were without arms. But Keith was not a man to hesitate long because of possible danger, and he stepped down into the shallow water.

"Come on, Neb," he commanded, "and we'll find out who lives here."

The window faced the west, and he came up the low bank to where the door fronted the north in intense darkness. Under the shadow of the cottonwoods he could see nothing, groping his way, with hands extended. His foot struck a flat stone, and he plunged forward, striking the unlatched door so heavily as to swing it open, and fell partially forward into the room. As he struggled to his knees, Neb's black face peering past him into the lighted interior, he seemed to perceive in one swift, comprehensive glance, every revealed detail. A lamp burned on a rudely constructed set of drawers near the window, and a wood fire blazed redly in a stone fireplace opposite, the yellow and red lights blending in a peculiar glow of color. Under this radiance were revealed the rough log walls, plastered with yellow clay, and hung about with the skins of wild animals, a roughly made table, bare except for a book lying upon it, and a few ordinary appearing boxes, evidently utilized as seats, together with a barrel cut so as to make a comfortable chair. In the back wall was a door, partially open, apparently leading into a second room. That was all, except the woman.

Keith must have perceived all these in that first hurried glance, for they were ever after closely associated together in his mind, yet at the moment he possessed

no clear thought of anything except her. She stood
directly behind the table, where she must have sprung
hastily at the first sound of their approach, clutching
at the rude mantel above the fireplace, and staring toward him, her face white, her breath coming in sobs.
At first he thought the vision a dream, a delirium born
from his long struggle; he could not conceive the possibility of such a presence in this lonely place, and
staggering to his feet, gazed wildly, dumbly at the
slender, gray clad figure, the almost girlish face under
the shadowing dark hair, expecting the marvellous vision to vanish. Surely this could not be real! A
woman, and such a woman as this here, and alone, of all
places! He staggered from weakness, almost terror,
and grasped the table to hold himself erect. The rising
wind came swirling in through the open door, causing
the fire to send forth spirals of smoke, and he turned,
dragging the dazed negro within, and snapping the
latch behind him. When he glanced around again he
fully believed the vision confronting him would have
vanished. But no! there she yet remained, those wide-
open, frightened brown eyes, with long lashes half hiding their depths, looking directly into his own; only
now she had slightly changed her posture, leaning toward him across the table. Like a flash he comprehended that this was reality — flesh and blood — and,

with the swift instinct of a gentleman, his numbed, nerveless fingers jerked off his hat, and he bowed bare-headed before her.

"Pardon me," he said, finding his voice with diffi-culty. "I fell over the step, but — but I did n't ex-pect to find a woman here."

He heard her quick breathing, marked a slight change in the expression of the dark eyes, and caught the glitter of the firelight on a revolver in her lowered hand.

"What did you expect to find?"

"I hardly knew," he explained lamely; "we stum-bled on this hut by accident. I did n't know there was a cabin in all this valley."

"Then you are not here for any purpose? to meet with any one?"

"No; we were lost, and had gone into camp up above, when we discovered your light."

"Where do you come from?"

Keith hesitated just an instant, yet falsehood was never easy for him, and he saw no occasion for any de-ceit now.

"Carson City."

"What brought you here?"

"We started for the 'Bar X' Ranch down below, on the Canadian; got caught in a sand-storm, and then just drifted. I do not know within twenty miles of where we are."

She drew a deep breath of unconcealed relief.

" Are you alone? "

" The negro and I — yes; and you have n't the slightest reason to be afraid of us — we 're square."

She looked at him searchingly, and something in Keith's clean-cut face seemed to bring reassurance, confidence in the man.

" I am not afraid," she answered, coming toward him around the short table. " Only it is so lonely here, and you startled me, bursting in without warning. But you look all right, and I am going to believe your story. What is your name? "

" Keith — Jack Keith."

" A cowman? "

" A little of everything, I reckon," a touch of returning bitterness in the tone. " A plainsman, who has punched cattle, but my last job was government scout."

" You look as though you might be more than that," she said slowly.

The man flushed, his lips pressing tightly together.

" Well, I — I may have been," he confessed unwillingly. " I started out all right, but somehow I reckon I just went adrift. It 's a habit in this country."

Apparently those first words of comment had left

her lips unthinkingly, for she made no attempt to reply; merely stood there directly facing him, her clear eyes gazing frankly into his own.  He seemed to actually see her now for the first time, fairly — a supple, slender figure, simply dressed, with wonderfully expressive brown eyes, a perfect wealth of dark hair, a clear complexion with slight olive tinge to it, a strong, intelligent face, not strictly beautiful, yet strangely attractive, the forehead low and broad, the nose straight, the lips full and inclined to smile.  Suddenly a vague remembrance brought recognition.

" Why, I know you now."

" Indeed! " the single word a note of undisguised surprise.

" Yes; I thought you looked oddly familiar all the time, but could n't for the life of me connect up. You 're Christie Maclaire."

" Am I ? " her eyes filled with curiosity.

" Of course you are.  You need n't be afraid of me if you want it kept secret, but I know you just the same. Saw you at the ' Gaiety ' in Independence, maybe two months ago.  I went three times, mostly on your account.  You 've got a great act, and you can sing too."

She stood in silence, still looking fixedly at him, her bosom rising and falling, her lips parted as if to speak.

Apparently she did not know what to do, how to act, and was thinking swiftly.

" Mr. Keith," she said, at last in decision, " I am going to ask you to blot that all out — to forget that you even suspect me of being Christie Maclaire, of the Gaiety."

" Why, certainly; but would you explain? "

" There is little enough to explain. It is sufficient that I am here alone with you. Whether I wish to or not, I am compelled to trust myself to your protection. You may call me Christie Maclaire, or anything else you please; you may even think me unworthy respect, but you possess the face of a gentleman, and as such I am going to trust you — I must trust you. Will you accept my confidence on these terms? "

Keith did not smile, nor move. Weak from hunger and fatigue, he leaned wearily against the wall. Nevertheless that simple, womanly appeal awoke all that was strong and sacrificing within him, although her words were so unexpected that, for the moment, he failed to realize their full purport. Finally he straightened up.

" I — I accept any terms you desire," he gasped weakly, " if — if you will only give one return."

" One return? — what? "

"Food; we have eaten nothing for sixty hours."

Her face, which had been so white, flushed to the hair, her dark eyes softening.

"Why, of course; sit down.   I ought to have known from your face.   There is plenty here — such as it is — only you must wait a moment."

# CHAPTER IX

### THE GIRL OF THE CABIN

HE saw Neb drop down before the blazing fire-place, and curl up like a tired dog, and observed her take the lamp, open the door into the other room a trifle, and slip silently out of sight. He remembered staring vaguely about the little room, still illumined by the flames, only half comprehending, and then the reaction from his desperate struggle with the elements overcame all resolution, and he dropped his head forward on the table, and lost consciousness. Her hand upon his shoulder aroused him, startled into wakefulness, yet he scarcely realized the situation.

"I have placed food for the negro beside him," she said quietly, and for the first time Keith detected the soft blur in her speech.

"You are from the South!" he exclaimed, as though it was a discovery.

"Yes — and you?"

"My boyhood began in Virginia — the negro was an old-time slave in our family."

6                        81

She glanced across at the black, now sitting up and eating voraciously.

"I thought he had once been a slave; one can easily tell that. I did not ask him to sit here because, if you do not object, we will eat here together. I have also been almost as long without food. It was so lonely here, and — and I hardly understood my situation — and I simply could not force myself to eat."

He distinguished her words clearly enough, although she spoke low, as if she preferred what was said between them should not reach the ears of the negro, yet somehow, for the moment, they made no adequate impression on him. Like a famished wolf he began on the coarse fare, and for ten minutes hardly lifted his head. Then his eyes chanced to meet hers across the narrow table, and instantly the gentleman within him reawoke to life.

"I have been a perfect brute," he acknowledged frankly, "with no thought except for myself. Hunger was my master, and I ask your forgiveness, Miss Maclaire."

Her eyes smiled.

"I am so very glad to have any one here — any one — in whom I feel even a little confidence — that nothing else greatly matters. Can you both eat, and listen?"

Keith nodded, his eyes full of interest, searching her face.

"Whoever I may be, Mr. Keith, and really that seems only of small importance, I came to Fort Larned seeking some trace of my only brother, whom we last heard from there, where he had fallen into evil companionship. On the stage trip I was fortunate enough to form an acquaintance with a man who told me he knew where I could meet Fred, but that the boy was hiding because of some trouble he had lately gotten into, and that I should have to proceed very carefully so as not to lead the officers to discover his whereabouts. This gentleman was engaged in some business at Carson City, but he employed a man to bring me to this place, and promised to get Fred, and meet me here the following day. There must have been some failure in the plans, for I have been here entirely alone now for three days. It has been very lonesome, and — and I 've been a little frightened. Perhaps I ought not to have come, and I am not certain what kind of a place this is. I was so afraid when you came, but I am not afraid now."

"You have no need to be," he said soberly, impressed by the innocent candor of the girl, and feeling thankful that he was present to aid her. "I could not wrong one of the South."

"My father always told me I could trust a Southern

gentleman under any circumstance. Mr. Hawley was from my own State, and knew many of our old friends. That was why I felt such unusual confidence in him, although he was but a travelling acquaintance."

" Mr. Hawley? "

" The gentleman whom I met on the stage."

" Oh, yes; you said he was in business in Carson City, but I don't seem to remember any one of that name."

" He was not there permanently; only to complete some business deal."

" And your brother? I may possibly have known him."

She hesitated an instant, her eyes dropping, until completely shaded by the long lashes.

" He — he was rather a wild boy, and ran away from home to enlist in the army. But he got into a bad set, and — and deserted. That was part of the trouble which caused him to hide. He enlisted under the name of Fred Willoughby. Mr. Hawley told me this much, but I am afraid he did not tell me all."

" And he said you would meet him here? "

Keith gazed about on the bare surroundings wonderingly. What was this place, hidden away in the midst of the desert, isolated in a spot where not even Indians roamed. Could it be a secret rendezvous of crime, the headquarters of desperadoes, of cattle-rustlers, of highwaymen of the Santa Fé Trail — a point to which they could ride when hard pressed, certain of hiding here in safety? He began to suspect this, but, if so, who then was this Hawley, and with what object had he sent this girl here? Every way he turned was to confront mystery, to face a new puzzle. Whatever she might be — even the music hall singer he believed — she had been inveigled here innocently enough. Even now she possessed only the most vague suspicion that she had been deceived. The centre of the whole plot, if there was a plot, must be Hawley.

"Yes," she replied, "he said that this was one of the stations of a big ranch on which Fred was employed, and that he would certainly be here within a day or two."

"You met Hawley on the stage coach? How did you become acquainted?"

"We were alone for nearly fifty miles," her voice faltering slightly, "and — and he called me what you did."

"Christie Maclaire?"

"Yes; he — he seemed to think he knew me, and I needed help so much that I let him believe so. I thought it could do no harm, and then, when I found he actually knew Fred, I did n't think of anything else, only how fortunate I was to thus meet him. Surely something serious must have happened, or he would have been here before this. Do you — do you suppose there is anything wrong?"

Keith did not smile nor change posture. The more he delved into the matter, the more serious he felt the situation to be. He knew all those ranches lying south on the Canadian, and was aware that this was no outstation. No cattle ever came across that sandy desert unless driven by rustlers, and no honest purpose could account for this isolated hut. There had been frequent robberies along the trail, and he had overheard tales of mysterious disappearances in both Larned and Carson City. Could it be that he had now, accidentally, stumbled upon the rendezvous of the gang? He was not a man easily startled, but this thought sent his heart beating. He knew enough to realize what such a gang would naturally consist of — deserters, outlaws, rustlers; both Indians and whites, no doubt, combined under some desperate leadership. Gazing into the girl's questioning eyes he could scarcely refrain from blurting out all he suspected. Yet why should he? What good could it do? He could not hope to bear her south to the "Bar X" Ranch, for the ponies were already too thoroughly exhausted for such a journey; he dared not turn north with her, for that would mean his own arrest, leaving her in worse condition than ever. If he only knew who this man Hawley was, his purpose, and plans! Yet what protection could he and Neb prove, alone here, and without arms? All this flashed through his mind in an instant, leaving him confused and uncertain.

" I hope not," he managed to say in answer to her query. " But it is rather a strange mix-up all around, and I confess I fail to comprehend its full meaning. It is hardly likely your friends will show up to-night, and by morning perhaps we can decide what is best to do. Let me look around outside a moment."

Her eyes followed him as he stepped through the door into the darkness; then her head dropped into the support of her hands. There was silence except for the crackling of the fire, until Neb moved uneasily. At the sound the girl looked up, seeing clearly the good-natured face of the negro.

" Yo' don't nebber need cry, Missus," he said soberly, " so long as Massa Jack done 'greed to look after yo'."

" Have — have you known him long? "

" Has I knowed him long, honey? Ebber sence befo' de wah. Why I done knowed Massa Jack when he wan't more'n dat high. Lawd, he sho' was a lively youngster, but mighty good hearted to us niggers."

She hesitated to question a servant, and yet felt she must uncover the truth.

"Who is he? Is he all he claims to be — a Virginia gentleman?"

All the loyalty and pride of slavery days was in Neb.

"He sho' am, Missus; dar ain't nuthin' higher in ol' Virginia dan de Keiths. Dey ain't got much money sence the Yankees come down dar, but dey 's quality folks jest de same. I was done born on de ol' Co'nel's plantation, and I reck'n dar wan't no finer man ebber libed. He was done killed in de wah. An' Massa Jack he was a captain; he rode on hossback, an' Lawdy, but he did look scrumptuous when he first got his uniform. He done fought all through de wah, an' dey say Ginral Lee done shook hands wid him, an' said how proud he was ter know him. You kin sutt'nly tie to Massa Jack, Missus."

The negro's voice had scarcely ceased when Keith came in again, closing the door securely behind him.

"All quiet outside," he announced, speaking with new confidence. "I wanted to get an understanding of the surroundings in case of emergency," he explained, as if in answer to the questioning of the brown eyes gravely uplifted to his face. "I see there is quite a corral at the lower end of this island, safely hidden behind the fringe of cottonwoods. And a log stable back of the house. Is the creek fordable both ways?"

"I think so; the man who brought me here rode away south."

"And are you going to trust yourself to my care?"

She came around the table with hands extended. He took them into his grasp, looking down into her eyes.

"Yes," she said softly, "I am going to trust you, Captain Keith."

He laughed.

"Captain, hey? You must have been talking with that black rascal there."

The swift color flooded her face, but her hands remained imprisoned.

"I just done tol' her who de Keiths was down in ol' Virginia, sah," burst in Neb indignantly. "I sho' don't want nobody to think I go trapsin' 'round wid any low white trash."

The gray eyes and the brown, gazing into one another, smiled with understanding.

"Oh, well," Keith acknowledged, genially, "I cannot say I am sorry you know something of my past glories; if one can't have a future, it is some source of pride to have a past to remember. But now about the present. We're not much protection to any one, the way we're fixed, as we are unarmed."

"There is a big revolver hanging in a holster in the other room," she answered, "and a short, sawed-off gun of some kind, but I don't know about ammunition."

"May we investigate?"

"Most certainly," and she threw open the intervening door. As the two stepped into the other apartment she held the lamp in aid of their search. "There is the revolver on the wall, and the gun is in the opposite corner. Isn't it strange you should be out in this country without arms?"

Keith glanced up, the revolver in his hands. The radiance of the light was full upon her face, revealing the clearness of her skin, the dark shadows of her lashes. There was the faintest tinge of suspicion to the question, but he answered easily.

"We left Carson in something of a hurry. I'll tell you the story to-morrow."

# CHAPTER X

## MR. HAWLEY REVEALS HIMSELF

A FRAGMENT of candle, stuck tightly into the neck of an empty bottle, appeared on a low shelf, and Keith lighted it, the girl returning the lamp to its former position on the front room table. Investigation revealed a dozen cartridges fitting the revolver, but no ammunition was discovered adapted to the sawed-off gun, which Neb had already appropriated, and was dragging about with him, peering into each black corner in anxious search. The two were still busily employed at this, when to their ears, through the stillness of the night, there came the unexpected noise of splashing in the water without, and then the sound of a horse stumbling as he struck the bank. Quick as a flash Keith closed the intervening door, extinguished the dim flame of the candle, and grasping the startled negro's arm, hushed him into silence.

Crouching close behind the door, through a crack of which the light streamed, yielding slight view of the interior, the plainsman anxiously awaited developments. These arrivals must certainly be some of those connected with the house; there could be little doubt as to that. Nevertheless, they might prove the posse following them, who had chanced to stumble accidentally on their retreat. In either case they could merely wait, and learn. Some one swore without, and was sharply rebuked by another voice, which added an order gruffly. Then the outer latch clicked, and a single man stepped within, immediately closing the door. Keith could not see the girl through the small aperture, but he heard her quick exclamation, startled, yet full of relief.

"Oh, is it you? I am so glad!"

The man laughed lightly.

"It is nice to be welcomed, although, perhaps, after your time of loneliness any arrival would prove a relief. Did you think I was never coming, Christie?"

"I could not understand," she replied, evidently with much less enthusiasm, and to Keith's thinking, a shade resentful of the familiarity, "but naturally supposed you must be unexpectedly delayed."

"Well, I was," and he apparently flung both coat and hat on a bench, with the intention of remaining. "The marshal arrested a fellow for a murder committed out on the Santa Fé Trail, and required me as a witness. But the man got away before we had any chance to try him, and I have been on his trail ever since."

"A murder!  Did you imagine he came this way?"

"Not very likely; fact of it is, the sand storm yesterday destroyed all traces, and, as a result, we've lost him.  So I headed a few of the boys over in this direction, as I wanted to relieve you of anxiety."

She was silent an instant, and the man crossed to the fireplace, where Keith could gain a glimpse of him. Already suspicious from the familiar sound of his voice, he was not surprised to recognize "Black Bart." The plainsman's fingers gripped the negro's arm, his eyes burning.  So this gambler and blackleg was the gentlemanly Mr. Hawley, was he; well, what could be his little game?  Why had he inveigled the girl into this lonely spot?  And what did he now propose doing with her?  As he crouched there, peering through that convenient crack in the door, Keith completely forgot his own peril, intent only upon this new discovery.  She came slowly around the end of the table, and stood leaning against it, her face clearly revealed in the light of the lamp.  For the first time Keith really perceived its beauty, its fresh charm. Could such as she be singer and dancer in a frontier concert hall?  And if so, what strange conditions ever drove her into that sort of life?

" Is — is Fred with you? " she questioned, doubt-fully.

" No; he 's with another party riding farther west," the man 's eyes surveying her with manifest approval. " You are certainly looking fine to-night, my girl. It 's difficult to understand how I ever managed to keep away from you so long."

She flushed to the hair, her lips trembling at the open boldness of his tone.

" I — I prefer you would not speak like that," she protested.

" And why not? " with a light laugh. " Come, Christie, such fine airs are a trifle out of place. If I did n't know you were a concert hall artist, I might be more deeply impressed. As it is, I reckon you 've heard love words before now."

" Mr. Hawley, I have trusted you as a gentleman. I never came here except on your promise to bring me to my brother," and she stood erect before him. " You have no right to even assume that I am Christie Maclaire."

" Sure not; I don't assume. I have seen that lady too often to be mistaken. Don't try on that sort of thing with me — I don't take to it kindly. Perhaps a kiss might put you in better humor."

He took a step forward, as though proposing to

carry out his threat, but the girl stopped him, her eyes burning with indignation.

"How dare you!" she exclaimed passionately, all fear leaving her in sudden resentment. "You think me alone here and helpless; that you can insult me at your pleasure. Don't go too far, Mr. Hawley. I know what you are now, and it makes no difference what you may think of me, or call me; you 'll find me perfectly able to defend myself."

"Oh, indeed!" sneeringly, "you are melodramatic; you should have been an actress instead of a singer. But you waste your talent out here on me. Do you imagine I fear either you, or your precious brother? Why, I could have him hung to-morrow."

She was staring at him with wide open eyes, her face white.

"What — what do you mean? What has Fred done?"

He was cold and sarcastic.

"That makes no difference; it is what I could induce men to swear he had done. It 's easy enough to convict in this country, if you only know how. I simply tell you this, so you won't press me too hard. Puritanism is out of place west of the Missouri, especially among ladies of your profession. Oh, come, now, Christie, don't try to put such airs on with me. I know who you are, all right, and can guess why you are hunting after Fred Willoughby. I pumped the boy, and got most of the truth out of him."

" You — you have seen him, then, since you left me," she faltered, bewildered, " and did n't bring him here with you?"

" Why should I ? " and the man stepped forward, his eyes on her, his hands twitching with a desire to clasp her to him, yet restrained by some undefinable power. " While I believed your brother story, I could have played the good Samaritan most beautifully, but after I talked with Willoughby I prefer him at a distance."

" My brother story! Do you mean to insinuate you doubt his being my brother? He told you that? "

" He gave up the whole trick. You can't trust a kid like that, Christie. A couple of drinks will loosen his tongue, and put you in wrong. Come, now, I know it all; be reasonable."

Apparently the girl had lost her power of speech, staring blindly at the face of the man before her, as a bird meets the slow approach of a snake. Keith could see her lips move, but making no sound. Hawley evidently interpreted her silence as hesitation, doubt as to his real meaning.

" You see where you are at now, Christie," he went on swiftly. " But you don't need to be afraid. I 'm going to be a friend to you, and you can be mighty glad you got rid of Willoughby so easily. Why, I can buy you diamonds where he could n't give you a calico dress. Come on, let 's stop this foolishness. I took a liking to you back there in the stage, and the more I 've thought about you since the crazier I 've got. When I succeeded in pumping Willoughby dry, and discovered you was n't his sister at all, why that settled the matter. I came down here after you. I love you, do you understand that? And, what 's more, I intend to have you!"

He reached out, and actually grasped her, but, in some manner, she tore loose, and sprang back around the end of the table, her cheeks flushed, her eyes burning.

" Don't touch me! don't dare touch me!" she panted. " You lie; Fred Willoughby never told you that. If you come one step nearer, I 'll scream; I 'll call your men here; I 'll tell them the kind of a cur you are."

He laughed, leaning over toward her, yet hesitating, his eyes full of admiration. Her very fierceness appealed to him, urged him on.

" Oh, I would n't! In the first place they probably

7

would n't hear, for they are camped down in the corral. I suspected you might be something of a tigress, and preferred to fight it out with you alone. Then, even if they did hear, there would be no interference — I 've got those fellows trained too well for that. Come on, Christie; you 're helpless here."

"Am I?"

"Yes, you are."

He took a step toward her, his hands flung out. With one quick movement she sprang aside and extinguished the lamp, plunging the room into instant darkness. A few red coals glowed dully in the fireplace, but all else was dense blackness. Keith heard the movements of Hawley, as he felt his way uncertainly along the table, swearing as he failed to find the girl. Then, like a shadow, he glided through the partly open door into the room.

# CHAPTER XI

## THE FIGHT IN THE DARK

HAD the room been filled with men Keith could have restrained himself no longer. Whatever her past might be, this woman appealed to him strangely; he could not believe evil of her; he would have died if need be in her defence. But as it was, the ugly boast of Hawley gave confidence in the final outcome of this struggle in the dark, even a possibility of escape for them all. The gambler, assured of being confronted merely by a frail and not over-scrupulous woman, had ventured there alone; had stationed his men beyond sound; had doubtless instructed them to ignore any noise of struggle which they might overhear within. It was these very arrangements for evil which now afforded opportunity, and Keith crept forward, alert and ready, his teeth clenched, his hands bare for contest. Even although he surprised his antagonist, it was going to be a fight for life; he knew "Black Bart," broad-shouldered, quick as a cat, accustomed to every form of physical exercise, desperate and tricky, using either knife or gun recklessly. Yet

99

it was now or never for all of them, and the plainsman felt no mercy, experienced no reluctance. He
reached the table, and straightened up, silent, expectant.
For an instant there was no further sound; no evidence of movement in the room. Hawley, puzzled
by the silence, was listening intently in an endeavor to
thus locate the girl through some rustling, some slight
motion. A knife, knocked from the table, perhaps,
as she slipped softly past, fell clattering to the floor,
and the gambler leaped instantly foward. Keith's
grip closed like iron on his groping arm, while he
shot one fist out toward where the man's head should
be. The blow glanced, yet drove the fellow backward, stumbling against the table, and Keith closed in,
grappling for the throat. The other, startled by the
unexpected attack, and scarcely realizing even yet the
nature of his antagonist, struggled blindly to escape
the fingers clawing at him, and flung one hand down to
the knife in his belt. Warned by the movement, the
assailant drove his head into the gambler's chest, send-
ing him crashing to the floor, falling himself heavily
upon the prostrate body. Hawley gave utterance to
one cry, half throttled in his throat, and then the two
grappled fiercely, so interlocked together as to make
weapons useless. Whoever the assailant might be, the
gambler was fully aware by now that he was being

crushed in the grasp of a fighting man, and exerted every wrestler's trick, every ounce of strength, to break free. Twice he struggled to his knees, only to be crowded backward by relentless power; once he hurled Keith sideways, but the plainsman's muscles stiffened into steel, and he gradually regained his position. Neither dared release a grip in order to strike a blow; neither had sufficient breath left with which to utter a sound. They were fighting for life, silently, desperately, like wild beasts, with no thought but to injure the other. The gambler's teeth sank into Keith's arm, and the latter in return jammed the man's head back onto the puncheon floor viciously. Perspiration streamed from their bodies, their fingers clutching, their limbs wrapped together, their muscles strained to the utmost. Keith had forgotten the girl, the negro, everything, dominated by the one passion to conquer. He was swept by a storm of hatred, a desire to kill. In their fierce struggle the two had rolled close to the fireplace, and in the dull glow of the dying embers, he could perceive a faint outline of the man's face. The sight added flame to his mad passion, yet he could do nothing except to cling to him, jabbing his fingers into the straining throat.

The negro ended the affair in his own way, clawing blindly at the combatants in the darkness, and finally, determining which was the enemy, he struck the gambler with the stock of his gun, laying him out unconscious. Keith, grasping the table, hauled himself to his feet, gasping for breath, certain only that Hawley was no longer struggling. For an instant all was blank, a mist of black vapor; then a realization of their situation came back in sudden flood of remembrance. Even yet he could see nothing, but felt the motionless figure at his feet.

"Quick," he urged, the instant he could make himself speak. "The fellow is only stunned; we must tie and gag him. Is that you, Neb? Where is the girl?"

"I am here, Captain Keith," and he heard the soft rustle of her dress across the room. "What is it I may do?"

"A coil of rope, or some straps, with a piece of cloth; anything you can lay hands on."

She was some moments at it, confused by the darkness, and Hawley moved slightly, his labored breathing growing plainly perceptible. Keith heard her groping toward him, and held out his hands. She started as he thus unexpectedly touched her, yet made no effort to break away.

"You — you frightened me a little," she confessed.

"This has all happened so quickly I hardly realize yet just what has occurred."

"The action has only really begun," he assured her, still retaining his hold upon her hand. "This was merely a preliminary skirmish, and you must prepare to bear your part in what follows. We have settled Mr. Hawley for the present, and now must deal with his gang."

"Oh, what would I have done if you had not been here?"

"Let us not think about that; we were here, and now have a busy night before us if we get away safely. Give me the rope first. Good! Here, Neb, you must know how to use this,— not too tight, but without leaving any play to the arms; take the knife out of his belt. Now for the cloth, Miss Maclaire."

"Please do not call me that!"

"But you said it did n't make any difference what I called you."

"I thought it did n't then, but it does now."

"Oh, I see; we are already on a new footing. Yet I must call you something."

She hesitated just long enough for him to notice it. Either she had no substitute ready at hand, or else doubted the advisability of confiding her real name under present circumstances to one so nearly a stranger.

"You may call me Hope."

"A name certainly of good omen," he returned. "From this moment I shall forget Christie Maclaire, and remember only Miss Hope. All right, Neb; now turn over a chair, and sit your man up against it. He will rest all the easier in that position until his gang arrive."

He thrust his head out of the door, peering cautiously forth into the night, and listening. A single horse, probably the one Hawley had been riding, was tied to a dwarfed cottonwood near the corner of the cabin. Nothing else living was visible.

"I am going to round up our horses, and learn the condition of Hawley's outfit," he announced in a low voice. "I may be gone for fifteen or twenty minutes, and, meanwhile, Miss Hope, get ready for a long ride. Neb, stand here close beside the door, and if any one tries to come in brain him with your gun-stock. I'll rap three times when I return."

He slipped out into the silent night, and crept cautiously around the end of the dark cabin. The distinct change in the girl's attitude of friendship toward him, her very evident desire that he should think well of her, together with the providential opportunity for escape, had left him full of confidence. The gambler had played blindly into their hands, and Keith was quick enough to accept the advantage. It was a risk to himself, to be sure, thus turning again to the northward, yet the clear duty he owed the girl left such a choice almost imperative. He certainly could not drag her along with him on his flight into the wild Comanche country extending beyond the Canadian. She must, at the very least, be first returned to the protection of the semi-civilization along the Arkansas. After that had been accomplished, he would consider his own safety. He wondered if Hope really was her name, and whether it was the family cognomen, or her given name. That she was Christie Maclaire he had no question, yet that artistic embellishment was probably merely assumed for the work of the concert hall. Both he and Hawley could scarcely be mistaken as to her identity in this respect, and, indeed, she had never openly denied the fact. Yet she did not at all seem to be that kind, and Keith mentally contrasted her with numerous others whom he had somewhat intimately known along the border circuit. It was difficult to associate her with that class; she must have come originally from some excellent family East, and been driven to the life by necessity; she was more to be pitied than blamed. Keith held no puri-

tanical views of life — his own experiences had been
too rough and democratic for that — yet he clung
tenaciously to an ideal of womanhood which could not
be lowered. However interested he might otherwise
feel, no Christie Maclaire could ever find entrance into
the deeps of his heart, where dwelt alone the memory
of his mother.

He found the other horses turned into the corral,
and was able, from their restless movements, to decide
they numbered eight. A fire, nearly extinguished,
glowed dully at the farther corner of the enclosure,
and he crawled close enough to distinguish the re-
cumbent forms of men sleeping about it on the ground.
Apparently no guard had been set, the fellows being
worn out from their long ride, and confident of safety
in this isolated spot. Besides, Hawley had probably
assumed that duty, and told them to get whatever sleep
they could. However, the gate of the corral opened
beside their fire, and Keith dare not venture upon rop-
ing any of their ponies, or leading them out past where
they slept. There might be clippers in the cabin with
which he could cut the wires, yet if one of the gang
awoke, and discovered the herd absent, it would result in an alarm, and lead to early pursuit. It was far
safer to use their own ponies. He would lead
Hawley's horse quietly through the water, and they

could mount on the other shore. This plan settled, he went at it swiftly, riding the captured animal while rounding up the others, and fastening the three to stunted trees on the opposite bank. Everything within the cabin remained exactly as he had left it, and he briefly explained the situation, examining Hawley's bonds again carefully while doing so.

"He'll remain there all right until his men find him," he declared, positively, "and that ought to give us a good six hours' start. Come, Miss Hope, every minute counts now."

He held her arm, not unconscious of its round shapeliness, as he helped her down the rather steep bank through the dense gloom. Then the two men joined hands, and carrying her easily between them, waded the shallow stream. The horses, not yet sufficiently rested to be frisky, accepted their burdens meekly enough, and, with scarcely a word spoken, the three rode away silently into the gloom of the night.

# CHAPTER XII

### THROUGH THE NIGHT SHADOWS

KEITH had very little to guide him, as he could not determine whether this mysterious cabin on the Salt Fork lay to east or west of the usual cattle trail leading down to the Canadian. Yet he felt reasonably assured that the general trend of the country lying between the smaller stream and the valley of the Arkansas would be similar to that with which he was already acquainted. It was merely a wild stretch of sandy desolation, across which their horses would leave scarcely any trail, and even that little would be quickly obliterated by the first puff of wind. As they drew in toward the river valley this plain would change into sand dunes, baffling and confusing, but no matter how hard they pressed forward, it must be daylight long before they could hope to reach these, and this would give him opportunity to spy out some familiar landmark which would guide them to the ford. Meanwhile, he must head as directly north as possible, trusting the horses to find footing.

It was plains instinct, or rather long training in the open, which enabled him to retain any true sense of direction, for beyond the narrow fringe of cottonwoods along the stream, nothing was visible, the eyes scarcely able even to distinguish where earth and sky met. They advanced across a bare level, without elevation or depression, yet the sand appeared sufficiently solid, so that their horses were forced into a swinging lope, and they seemed to fairly press aside the black curtain, which as instantly swung shut once more, and closed them in. The pounding hoofs made little noise, and they pressed steadily onward, closely bunched together, so as not to lose each other, dim, spectral shadows flitting through the night, a very part of that grim desolation surrounding them. No one of the three felt like speaking; the gloomy, brooding desert oppressed them, their vagrant thoughts assuming the tinge of their surroundings; their hope centred on escape. Keith rode, grasping the rein of the woman's horse in his left hand, and bending low in vain effort at picking a path. He had nothing to aim toward, yet sturdy confidence in his expert plainscraft yielded him sufficient sense of direction. He had noted the bark of the cottonwoods, the direction of the wind, and steered a course accordingly straight northward, alert to avert any variation.

The girl rode easily, although in a man's saddle, the stirrups much too long.   Keith glanced aside with swift approval at the erectness with which she sat, the loosened rein in her hand, the slight swaying of her form.   He could appreciate horsemanship, and the easy manner in which she rode relieved him of one anxiety.   It even caused him to break the silence.

" You are evidently accustomed to riding, Miss Hope."

She glanced across at him through the darkness, as though suddenly surprised from thought, her words not coming quickly.

" I cannot remember when I first mounted a horse; in earliest childhood, surely, although I have not ridden much of late.   This one is like a rocking chair."

" He belonged to your friend, Mr. Hawley."

She drew a quick breath, her face again turned forward.

" Who — who is that man?   Do you know? "

" I possess a passing acquaintance," he answered, uncertain yet how much to tell her, but tempted to reveal all in test of her real character.   " Few do not who live along the Kansas border."

" Do you mean he is a notoriously bad character? "

" I have never heard of his being held up as a model to the young, Miss Hope," he returned more soberly, convinced that she truly possessed no real knowledge regarding the man, and was not merely pretending innocence. "I had never heard him called Hawley before, and, therefore, failed to recognize him under that respectable name. But I knew his voice the moment he entered the cabin, and realized that some devilment was afoot. Every town along this frontier has his record, and I 've met him maybe a dozen times in the past three years. He is known as ' Black Bart '; is a gambler by profession, a desperado by reputation, and a cur by nature. Just now I suspect him of being even deeper in the mire than this."

He could tell by the quick clasping of her hands on the pommel of the saddle the effect of his words, but waited until the silence compelled her to speak.

" Oh, I did n't know! You do not believe that I ever suspected such a thing? That I ever met him there understanding who he was? "

" No, I do not," he answered. " What I overheard between you convinced me you were the victim of deceit. But your going to that place alone was a most reckless act."

She lifted her hand to her eyes, her head drooping forward.

" Was n't it what he told me — the out-station of a ranch? "

" No; I have ridden this country for years, and there is no ranch pasturing cattle along the Salt Fork.   Miss Hope, I want you to comprehend what it is you have escaped from; what you are now fleeing from.   Within the last two years an apparently organized body of outlaws have been operating throughout this entire region.   Oftentimes disguised as Indians, they have terrorized the Santa Fé trail for two hundred miles, killing travellers in small parties, and driving off stock. There are few ranches as far west as this, but these have all suffered from raids.   These fellows have done more to precipitate the present Indian war than any act of the savages.   They have endeavored to make the authorities believe that Indians were guilty of their deeds of murder and robbery.   Both troops and volunteers have tried to hold the gang up, but they scatter and disappear, as though swallowed by the desert.   I have been out twice, hard on their trail, only to come back baffled.   Now, I think accident has given me the clue."

She straightened up; glancing questioningly at him through the darkness.

" That is what I mean, Miss Hope.   I suspect that cabin to be the rendezvous of those fellows, and I half believe Hawley to be their leader."

" Then you will report all this to the authorities? "

He smiled grimly, his lips compressed.

"I hardly think so; at least, not for the present.   I am not blood-thirsty, or enamored of man-hunting, but I happen to have a personal interest in this particular affair which I should prefer to settle alone." He paused, swiftly reviewing the circumstances of their short acquaintance, and as suddenly determining to trust her discretion.   Deep down in his heart he rather wanted her to know.   "The fact of the matter is, that Neb and I here were the ones that particular posse were trailing."

"You!" her voice faltered.   "He said those men were under arrest for murder, and had broken jail."

"He also said it was easy to convict men in this country if you only knew how.   It is true we broke jail, but only in order to save our lives; it was the only way.   Technically, we are outlaws, and now run the risk of immediate re-arrest by returning north of the Arkansas.   We came to you fugitives; I was charged with murder, the negro with assault.   So, you see, Miss Hope, the desperate class of men you are now associating with."

The slight bitterness in his tone stung the girl into resentment.   She was looking straight at him, but in the gloom he could not discern the expression of her eyes.

8

" I don't believe it," she exclaimed decisively, " you
— you do not look like that! "

" My appearance may be sufficient to convince you,"
he returned, rather dryly, " but would weigh little before
a Western court. Unfortunately, the evidence was
strong against me; or would have been had the case ever
come to a trial. The strange thing about it was that
both warrants were sworn out by the same complain-
ant, and apparently for a similar purpose —' Black
Bart ' Hawley."

" What purpose? "

" To keep us from telling what we knew regarding a
certain crime, in which either he, or some of his inti-
mate friends, were deeply interested."

" But it would all come out at the trial, wouldn't
it? "

" There was to be no trial; Judge Lynch settles the
majority of such cases out here at present. It is extremely simple. Listen, and I will tell you the story."

He reviewed briefly those occurrences leading directly
up to his arrest, saying little regarding the horrors of
that scene witnessed near the Cimmaron Crossing, but
making sufficiently clear his very slight connection with
it, and the reason those who were guilty of the crime
were so anxious to get him out of the way. She listened
intently, asking few questions, until he ended. Then

they both looked up, conscious that dawn was becoming
gray in the east. Keith's first thought was one of relief
— the brightening sky showed him they were riding
straight north.

# CHAPTER XIII

### THE FORD OF THE ARKANSAS

THEY were still in the midst of the yellow feature-
less plain, but the weary horses had slowed down
to a walk, the heavy sand retarding progress. It was
a gloomy, depressing scene in the spectral gray light,
a wide circle of intense loneliness, unbroken by either
dwarfed shrub or bunch of grass, a barren expanse
stretching to the sky. Vague cloud shadows seemed to
flit across the level surface, assuming fantastic shapes,
but all of the same dull coloring, imperfect and un-
finished. Nothing seemed tangible or real, but rather
some grotesque picture of delirium, ever merging into
another yet more hideous. The very silence of those
surrounding wastes seemed burdensome, adding im-
measurably to the horror. They were but specks crawl-
ing underneath the sky — the only living, moving ob-
jects in all that immense circle of desolation and death.

Keith turned in the saddle, looking back past Neb
— who swayed in his seat, with head lolling on his
breast as though asleep, his horse plodding after the
others — along the slight trail they had made across

the desert. So far as eye could reach nothing moved, nothing apparently existed. Fronting again to the north he looked upon the same grim barrenness, only that far off, against the lighter background of distant sky, there was visible a faint blur, a bluish haze, which he believed to be the distant sand dunes bordering the Arkansas. The intense dreariness of it all left a feeling of depression. His eyes turned and regarded the girl riding silently beside him. The same look of depression was visible upon her face, and she was gazing off into the dull distance with lack-lustre eyes, her slender form leaning forward, her hands clasped across the pommel. The long weariness of the night had left traces on her young face, robbing it of some of its freshness, yet Keith found it more attractive in the growing daylight than amid the lamp shadows of the evening before. He had not previously realized the peculiar clearness of her complexion, the rose tint showing through the olive skin, or the soft and silky fineness of her hair, which, disarranged, was strangely becoming under the broad brim of the hat she wore, drawn low until it shadowed her eyes. It was not a face to be easily associated with frontier concert halls, or any surrender to evil; the chin round and firm, the lips full, yet sufficiently compressed; the whole expression that of pure and dignified womanhood. She puzzled him, and he scarcely knew what to believe, or exactly how to act toward her.

"Our friends back yonder should be turning out from the corral by now," he said finally, anxious to break the silence, for she had not spoken since he ended his tale. "It will not be long until they discover Hawley's predicament, and perhaps the welkin already rings with profanity. That may even account for the blue haze out yonder."

She turned her eyes toward him, and the slightest trace of a smile appeared from out the depths of their weariness.

"If they would only remain satisfied with that. Will they follow us, do you think? And are we far enough away by this time to be safe?"

"It is hardly likely they will let us escape without a chase," he answered slowly. "We possess too much information now that we have their rendezvous located, and 'Black Bart' will have a private grudge to revenge. I wonder if he suspects who attacked him! But don't worry, Miss Hope; we have miles the start, and the wind has been strong enough to cover our trail. Do you see that dark irregularity ahead?"

"Yes; is it a cloud?"

"No; the Arkansas sand dunes. I am going to try to keep the horses moving until we arrive there.

Then we will halt and eat whatever Neb has packed behind him, and rest for an hour or two. You look very tired, but I hope you can keep up for that distance. We shall be safely out of sight then."

"Indeed, I am tired; the strain of waiting alone in that cabin, and all that happened last night, have tried me severely. But — but I can go through."

Her voice proved her weakness, although it was determined enough, and Keith, yielding to sudden impulse, put out his hand, and permitted it to rest upon hers, clasped across the pommel. Her eyes drooped, but there was no change of posture.

"Your nerve is all right," he said, admiringly, "you have shown yourself a brave girl."

"I could not be a coward, and be my father's daughter," she replied, with an odd accent of pride in her choking voice, "but I have been afraid, and — and I am still."

"Of what? Surely, not that those fellows will ever catch up with us?"

"No, I hardly know what, only there is a dread I cannot seem to shake off, as if some evil impended, the coming of which I can feel, but not see. Have you ever experienced any such premonition?"

He laughed, withdrawing his hand.

"I think not. I am far too prosaic a mortal to allow

dreams to worry me. So far I have discovered sufficient trouble in real life to keep my brain active. Even now I cannot forget how hungry I am."

She did not answer, comprehending how useless it would be to explain, and a little ashamed of her own ill-defined fears, and thus they rode on in silence. He did not notice that she glanced aside at him shyly, marking the outline of his clear-cut features, silhouetted against the far-off sky. It was a manly face, strong, alive, full of character, the well-shaped head firmly poised, the broad shoulders squared in spite of the long night of weary exertion. The depths of her eyes brightened with appreciation.

" I believe your story, Mr. Keith," she said at last softly.

" My story? " questioningly, and turning instantly toward her.

" Yes; all that you have told me about what happened."

" Oh; I had almost forgotten having told it, but I never felt any doubt but what you would believe. I don't think I could lie to you."

It was no compliment, but spoken with such evident honesty that her eyes met his with frankness.

" There could be no necessity; only I wanted you to know that I trust you, and am grateful."

She extended her hand this time, and he took it within his own, holding it firmly, yet without knowing what to answer. There was strong impulse within him to question her, to learn then and there her own life story. Yet, somehow, the reticence of the girl restrained him; he could not deliberately probe beneath the veil she kept lowered between them. Until she chose to lift it herself voluntarily, he possessed no right to intrude. The gentlemanly instincts of younger years held him silent, realizing clearly that whatever secret might dominate her life, it was hers to conceal just so long as she pleased. Out of this swift struggle of repression he managed to say:

" I appreciate your confidence, and mean to prove worthy. Perhaps some day I can bring you the proofs."

" I need none other than your own word."

" Oh, but possibly you are too easily convinced; you believed in Hawley."

She looked at him searchingly, her eyes glowing, her cheeks flushed.

" Yes," she said slowly, convincingly. " I know I did; I — I was so anxious to be helped, but — but this is different."

It was noon, the sun pitiless and hot above them, before they straggled within the partial shelter of the sand dunes, and sank wearily down to their meagre lunch. Their supply of water was limited, and the exhausted ponies must wait until they reached the river to quench their thirst. Yet this was not very far off now, and Keith had seen enough of their surroundings to locate the position of the ford. Slow as they must proceed, three hours more would surely bring them to the bank of the stream. They discussed their plans briefly as the three sat together on the warm sand, revived both by the food and the brief rest. There was not a great deal to be determined, only where the girl should be left, and how the two men had better proceed to escape observation.

Fort Larned was the nearest and safest place for their charge, none of the party expressing any desire to adventure themselves within the immediate neighborhood of Carson City. What her future plans might be were not revealed, and Keith forebore any direct questioning. His duty plainly ended with placing her in a safe environment, and he felt convinced that Mrs. Murphy, of the Occidental Hotel, would furnish room, and, if necessary, companionship. The sole problem remaining — after she had rather listlessly agreed to such an arrangement — was to so plan the details as to permit the negro and himself to slip through the small town clustered about the post without attracting undue attention.  No doubt, the story of their escape had already reached there, embellished by telling, and serious trouble might result from discovery. Keith was surprised at the slight interest she exhibited in these arrangements, merely signifying her acquiescence by a word, but he charged it to physical weariness, and the reaction from her night of peril; yet he took pains to explain fully his plan, and to gain her consent.

This finally settled, they mounted again and rode on through the lanes traversing the sand dunes, keeping headed as straight as possible toward the river.  The ford sought was some miles down stream, but with the horses' thirst mitigated, they made excellent progress, and arrived at the spot early in the evening.  Not in all the day had they encountered a living object, or seen a moving thing amid the surrounding desolation.  Now, looking across to the north, a few gleaming lights told of Fort Larned perched upon the opposite bluffs.

# CHAPTER XIV

## THE LANDLADY OF THE OCCIDENTAL

KEITH had crossed at this point so frequently with cattle that, once having his bearings, the blackness of the night made very little difference. Nevertheless, in fear lest her pony might stumble over some irregularity, he gave his own rein to Neb, and went forward on foot, grasping firmly the tired animal's bit. It was a long stretch of sand and water extending from bank to bank, but the latter was shallow, the only danger being that of straying off from the more solid bottom into quicksand. With a towering cottonwood as guide, oddly misshapen and standing out gauntly against the slightly lighter sky, the plainsman led on unhesitatingly, until they began to climb the rather sharp uplift of the north bank. Here there was a plain trail, pounded into smoothness by the hoofs of cavalry horses ridden down to water, and at the summit they emerged within fifty yards of the stables.

The few lights visible, some stationary, with others dancing about like will-o'-the-wisps, revealed imperfectly the contour of various buildings, but Keith turned sharply to the right, anxious to slip past without being challenged by a sentry.  Beyond the brow of the bluff other lights now became visible, flickering here and there, marking where a straggling town had sprung up under the protection of the post — a town garish enough in the daylight, composed mostly of shacks and tents, but now with its deficiencies mercifully concealed by the enveloping darkness.  The trail, easily followed, led directly along its single street, but Keith circled the outskirts through a wilderness of tin-cans and heaps of other debris, until he halted his charges beside the black shadow of the only two-story edifice in the place. This was the Occidental, the hospitality of which he had frequently tested.

A light streamed from out the front windows, but, uncertain who might be harbored within, Keith tapped gently at the back door.  It was not opened immediately, and when it was finally shoved aside the merest crack, no glow of light revealed the darkened interior.  The voice which spoke, however, was amply sufficient to identify its owner.

" Is that ye agin, Murphy, a playin' av yer dirthy thricks? "

" No, Mrs. Murphy," he hastened to explain, " this is Keith — Jack Keith, of the ' Bar X.' "

" The Lord deliver us! " was the instant exclamation, the door opening wide. "They do be afther tellin' me to-night av the throuble ye was in over at Carson, an' Oi t'ought maybe ye moight turn up this way. It was a nate thrick ye played on the loikes av 'em, Jack, but this is a dom poor place fer ye ter hide in. Bedad, there's a half-dozen in the parly now talkin' about it, wid a couple av officers from the fort. Is the nager wid ye?"

"Yes, but we have no intention of hiding here. I'd rather take my chance in the open. The fact is, Kate, we started off for the 'Bar X.'"

"Av course, ye did; Oi was shure av it."

"But down on the Salt Fork we ran across a young girl whom Black Bart had inveigled down that way on a lie. We had a bit of a fight, and got her away from him. This is what brought us back here — to put the girl where she will be safe out of his clutches."

The door was wide open now, and Mrs. Murphy outside, her interest at fever heat.

"Ye had a foight wid Black Bart! Oh, ye divil! An' ye licked the dirthy spalpane, an' got away wid his gyurl! Glory be! And would Oi take her? Well, Oi would. Niver doubt that, me bye. She may be the quane av Shaba, an' she may be a Digger Injun Squaw, but the loikes av him had betther kape away from Kate

Murphy. It 's glad Oi am ter do it! Bring her in. Oi don't want ter hear no more."

"Just a word, Kate; I don't know whether she has any money or not, but I 'll pay her bill, as soon as it is safe for me to come back."

"Oh, the divil take her bill. She 'll have the best in the house, annyhow, an' Oi 'm only hopin' that fellow will turn up huntin' her. Oi 'd loike ter take one slap at the spalpane."

Fully convinced as to Mrs. Murphy's good-will, Keith slipped back into the darkness, and returned with the girl. Introductions were superfluous, as the mistress of the Occidental cared little regarding ceremony.

"An' is this you, my dear?" she burst out, endeavoring to curb her voice to secretive softness. "Shure, Jack Keith has told me all about it, an' it 's safe it is yer goin' ter be here. Come on in; Oi 'll give ye number forty-two, thet 's next behint me own room, an' we 'll go up the back sthairs. Hilp the young loidy, Jack, fer shure ye know the way."

She disappeared, evidently with some hospitable purpose in view, and Keith, clasping the girl's hand, undertook the delicate task of safely escorting her through the dark kitchen, and up the dimly remembered stairs. Only a word or two passed between them, but as they neared the second story a light suddenly streamed out through the opened door of a room at their left. Mrs. Murphy greeted them at the landing, and for the first time saw the girl's weary white face, her eyes filled with appeal, and the warm Irish heart responded instantly.

"Ye poor little lamb; it's the bid ye want, an' a dhrap o' whiskey. Jack Keith, why did n't ye till me she was done up wid the hard ride? Here, honey, sit down in the rocker till Oi get ye a wee dhrink. It 'll bring the roses back to the cheeks av ye." She was gone, bustling down the dark stairs, and the two were alone in the room, the girl looking up into his face, her head resting against the cushioned back of the chair. He thought he saw a glimmer of tears in the depths of her lash-shaded eyes, and her round white throat seemed to choke.

"You will be perfectly secure here," he said, soothingly, "and can remain as long as you please. Mrs. Murphy will guard you as though you were her own daughter. She is a bit rough, maybe, but a big-hearted woman, and despises Hawley. She nursed me once through a touch of typhoid — yes, by Jove," glancing about in sudden recognition, "and in this very room, too."

The girl's glance wandered over the plain, neat furnishings, and the rather pathetic attempts at decoration, yet with apparently no thought for them.

" You — you have not told me where you were going."

He laughed, a little uneasily, as though he preferred to make light of the whole matter.

" Really, I have hardly decided, the world is so wide, and I had no reason to suppose you interested."

" But I am interested," resenting his tone of assumed indifference. " I would not want to feel that our acquaintance was to wholly end now."

" Do you really mean that? "

" Why should I not? You have been a real friend to me; I shall remember you always with a gratitude beyond words. I want you to know this, and that — that I shall ever wish to retain that friendship."

Keith struggled with himself, doubtful of what he had best say, swayed by unfamiliar emotions.

" You may be sure I shall never forget," he blurted forth, desperately, " and, if you really wish it, I 'll certainly see you again."

" I do," earnestly.

" Then, I 'll surely find a way. I don't know now which direction we will ride, but I 'm not going very far until I clear up that murder out yonder on the trail; that is my particular job just now."

9

Before she could answer, Mrs. Murphy reëntered, and forced her to drink the concoction prepared, the girl accepting with smiling protest. The landlady, empty glass in hand, swept her eyes about the room.

" Bedad, but the place looks betther than iver Oi 'd belaved, wid the gyurl Oi 've got tindin' to it. She 's that lazy she goes ter slape swapin' the flure. Jack, would ye moind hilpin' me move the bid; shure, it 's rale mahogany, an' so heavy it breaks me back intoirely to push it 'round."

He took hold willingly enough, and the two together ran the heavy contrivance across the room to the position selected. Once a leg caught in the rag carpet, and Keith lifted it out, bending low to get a firmer grip. Then he held out his hand to the girl.

" It is not going to be good-bye then, Miss Hope; I 'll find you."

She smiled up into his eyes, much of the weariness gone from her face.

" I am going to believe that," she answered, gladly, " because I want to."

Mrs. Murphy lingered until his steps sounded on the stairs, as he slowly felt his way down through the darkness.

" He do be a moighty foine bye, Jack Keith," she said, apparently addressing the side wall. " Oi wish

Oi 'd a knowed him whin Oi was a gyurl; shure, it's
not Murphy me noime 'd be now, Oi 'm t'inkin'."

Left alone, the girl bowed her head on her hands,
a hot tear stealing down through her fingers.  As she
glanced up again, something that glittered on the floor
beside the bed caught her eyes.  She stopped and picked
it up, holding the trinket to the light, staring at it as
though fascinated.  It was the locket Keith had taken
from the neck of the dead man at Cimmaron Crossing.
Her nerveless fingers pressed the spring, and the painted
face within looked up into her own, and still clasping
it within her hand, she sank upon her knees, burying
her face on the bed.

"Where did he get that?" her lips kept repeating.
"Where did he ever get that?"

# CHAPTER XV

## AGAIN CHRISTIE MACLAIRE

KEITH possessed sufficient means for several months of idleness, and even if he had not, his reputation as a plains scout would insure him employment at any of the more important scattered army posts. Reliable men for such service were in demand. The restlessness of the various Indian tribes, made specially manifest by raids on the more advanced settlements, and extending over a constantly widening territory, required continuous interchange of communication between commanders of detachments. Bold and reckless spirits had flocked to the frontier in those days following the Civil War, yet all were not of the type to encourage confidence in military authorities. Keith had already frequently served in this capacity, and abundantly proved his worth under rigorous demands of both endurance and intelligence, and he could feel assured of permanent employment whenever desired. Not a few of the more prominent officers he had met personally during the late war — including Sheridan, to whom he had once borne a flag of truce, — yet the spirit of the Confederacy still lingered in his heart: not in any feeling of either hatred or revenge, but in an unwillingness to serve the blue uniform, and a memory of antagonism which would not entirely disappear. He had surrendered at Appomattox, conquered, yet he could not quite adjust himself to becoming companion-in-arms with those against whom he had fought valiantly for four years. Some of the wounds of that conflict still smarted. A natural soldier, anxious to help the harassed settlers, eager enough to be actively employed, he still held aloof from army connections except as a volunteer in case of emergency.

Just now other considerations caused him to desire freedom. He had been accused of murder, imprisoned for it, and in order to escape, had been compelled to steal horses, the most heinous crime of the frontier. Not only for his own protection and safety must the truth of that occurrence at the Cimmaron Crossing be made clear, but he also had now a personal affair with " Black Bart " Hawley to be permanently settled. They had already clashed twice, and Keith intended they should meet again.

Memory of the girl was still in his mind as he and Neb rode silently forth on the black prairie, leading the extra horse behind them. He endeavored to drive the recollection from his mind, so he might concentrate it upon plans for the future, but somehow she mysteriously wove her own personality into those plans, and he was ever seeing the pleading in her eyes, and listening to the soft Southern accent of her voice. Of late years he had been unaccustomed to association with women of high type, and there was that touch of the gentlewoman about this girl which had awakened deep interest. Of course he knew that in her case it was merely an inheritance of her past, and could not truly represent the present Christie Maclaire of the music halls. However fascinating she might be, she could not be worthy any serious consideration. In spite of his rough life the social spirit of the old South was implanted in his blood, and no woman of that class could hold him captive. Yet, some way, she refused to be banished or left behind. Even Neb must have been obsessed by a similar spirit, for he suddenly observed:

" Dat am sutt'nly a mighty fine gal, Massa Jack. I ain't seen nothin' to compare wid her since I quit ol' Virginia —'deed I ain't."

Keith glanced back at his black satellite, barely able to distinguish the fellow's dim outlines.

" You think her a lady, then? " he questioned, giving thoughtless utterance to his own imagination.

" 'Deed I does! " the thick voice somewhat indignant. " I reck'n I knows de real quality when I sees it. I 'se 'sociated wid quality white folks befo'."

" But, Neb, she 's a singer in dance halls."

" I don't believe it, Massa Jack."

" Well, I would n't if I could help it. She don't seem like that kind, but I recognized her as soon as I got her face in the light. She was at the Gaiety in Independence, the last time I was there. Hawley knew her too, and called her by name."

Neb rubbed his eyes, and slapped his pony's flank, unable to answer, yet still unconvinced.

" I reck'n both ob yer might be mistook," he insisted doggedly.

" Not likely," and Keith's brief laugh was not altogether devoid of bitterness. " We both called her Christie Maclaire, and she did n't even deny the name; she was evidently not proud of it, but there was no denial that she was the girl."

" Dat was n't like no name dat you called her when we was ridin'."

" No; she did n't approve of the other, and told me to call her Hope, but I reckon she 's Christie Maclaire all right."

They rode on through the black, silent night as rapidly as their tired horses would consent to travel.

Keith led directly across the open prairie, guiding his course by the stars, and purposely avoiding the trails, where some suspicious eye might mark their passage. His first object was to get safely away from the scattered settlements lying east of Carson City. Beyond their radius he could safely dispose of the horses they rode, disappear from view, and find time to develop future plans. As to the girl — well, he would keep his word with her, of course, and see her again sometime. There would be no difficulty about that, but otherwise she should retain no influence over him. She belonged rather to Hawley's class than his.

It was a lonely, tiresome ride, during which Neb made various efforts to talk, but finding his white companion uncommunicative, at last relapsed into rather sullen silence. The horses plodded on steadily, and when daylight finally dawned, the two men found themselves in a depression leading down to the Smoky River. Here they came to a water hole, where they could safely hide themselves and their stock. With both Indians and white men to be guarded against, they took all the necessary precautions, picketing the horses closely under the rock shadows, and not venturing upon building any fire. Neb threw himself on the turf and was instantly asleep, but Keith climbed the steep side of the gully, and made searching survey of the horizon. The wide arc

to south, east, and west revealed nothing to his searching eyes, except the dull brown of the slightly rolling
plains, with no life apparent save some distant grazing antelope, but to the north extended more broken
country with a faint glimmer of water between the
hills.    Satisfied they were unobserved, he slid back again
into the depression.    As he turned to lie down he took
hold of the saddle belonging to Hawley's horse.    In
the unbuckled holster his eye observed the glimmer of
a bit of white paper.    He drew it forth, and gazed at it
unthinkingly.    It was an envelope, robbed of its contents, evidently not sent through the mails as it had not
been stamped, but across its face was plainly written,
" Miss Christie Maclaire."    He stared at it, his lips
firm set, his gray eyes darkening.    If he possessed any
doubts before as to her identity, they were all thoroughly
dissipated now.

.        .        .        .        .        .

As he lay there, with head pillowed on the saddle,
his body aching from fatigue yet totally unable to
sleep, staring open-eyed into the blue of the sky, the girl
they had left behind awoke from uneasy slumber,
aroused by the entrance of Mrs. Murphy.    For an instant she failed to comprehend her position, but the
strong brogue of the energetic landlady broke in
sharply:

"A bit av a cup av coffee fer ye, honey," she explained, crossing to the bed. "Shure an' there's nuthin' loike it when ye first wake up. Howly Mither, but it's toird 'nough ye do be lookin' yet."

"I have n't slept very well," the girl confessed, bringing her hand out from beneath the coverlet, the locket still tightly clasped in her fingers. "See, I found this on the floor last night after you had gone down stairs."

"Ye did!" setting the coffee on a convenient chair, and reaching out for the trinket. "Let's have a look at it once. Angels av Hiven, if it is n't the same the ol' Gineral was showin' me in the parly."

The other sat up suddenly, her white shoulders and rounded throat gleaming.

"The old General, you said? What General? When was he here?"

"Shure now, be aisy, honey, an' Oi 'll tell ye all there is to it. It's not his name Oi know; maybe Oi niver heard till av it, but 't was the 'Gineral' they called him, all right. He was here maybe three days outfittin'— a noice spoken ol' gintlemin, wid a gray beard, an' onc't he showed me the locket — be the powers, if it do be his, there's an openin' to it, an' a picter inside."

The girl touched the spring, revealing the face

within, but her eyes were blinded with tears. The landlady looked at her in alarm.

"What is it, honey? What is it? Did you know him?"

The slender form swayed forward, shaken with sobs.

"He was my father, and — and this is my mother's picture which he always carried."

"Then what is your name?"

"Hope Waite."

Kate Murphy looked at the face half hidden in the bed-clothes. That was not the name which Keith had given her, but she had lived on the border too long to be inquisitive. The other lifted her head, flinging back her loosened hair with one hand.

"Mr. Keith dropped it," she exclaimed. "Where do you suppose he got it?" Then she gave a quick, startled cry, her eyes opening wide in horror. "The Cimmaron Crossing, the murder at the Cimmaron Crossing! He — he told me about that; but he never showed me this — this. Do you — do you think —"

Her voice failed, but Kate Murphy gathered her into her arms.

"Cry here, honey," she said, as if to a child. "Shure an' Oi don't know who it was got kilt out yonder, but Oi 'm tellin' ye it niver was Jack Keith what did it — murther ain't his stoyle."

# CHAPTER XVI

### INTRODUCING DOCTOR FAIRBAIN

HEADED as they were, and having no other special objective point in view, it was only natural
for the two fugitives to drift into Sheridan. This was
at that time the human cesspool of the plains country,
a seething, boiling maelstrom of all that was rough,
evil, and brazen along the entire frontier. Customarily quiet enough during the hours of daylight, the
town became a mad saturnalia with the approach of
darkness, its ceaseless orgies being noisily continued
until dawn. But at this period all track work on the
Kansas Pacific being temporarily suspended by Indian
outbreaks, the graders made both night and day alike
hideous, and the single dirty street which composed
Sheridan, lined with shacks, crowded with saloons, the
dull dead prairie stretching away on every side to the
horizon, was congested with humanity during every
hour of the twenty-four.

It was a grim picture of depravity and desolation,
the environment dull, gloomy, forlorn; all that was
worthy the eye or thought being the pulsing human

element. All about extended the barren plains, except where on one side a ravine cut through an overhanging ridge. From the seething street one could look up to the summit, and see there the graves of the many who had died deaths of violence, and been borne thither in "their boots." Amid all this surrounding desolation was Sheridan — the child of a few brief months of existence, and destined to perish almost as quickly — the centre of the grim picture, a mere cluster of rude, unpainted houses, poorly erected shacks, grimy tents flapping in the never ceasing wind swirling across the treeless waste, the ugly red station, the rough cow-pens filled with lowing cattle, the huge, ungainly stores, their false fronts decorated by amateur wielders of the paint brush, and the garish dens of vice tucked in every-where. The pendulum of life never ceased swing-ing. Society was mixed; no man cared who his neigh-bor was, or dared to question. Of women worthy the name there were few, yet there were flitting female forms in plenty, the saloon lights revealing powdered cheeks and painted eyebrows. It was a strange, restless populace, the majority here to-day, disappearing to-mor-row — cowboys, half-breeds, trackmen, graders, des-peradoes, gamblers, saloon-keepers, merchants, gen-erally Jewish, petty officials, and a riff-raff no one could account for, mere floating debris. The town was an eddy catching odd bits of driftwood such as only the frontier ever knew. Queer characters were everywhere, wrecks of dissipation, derelicts of the East, seeking nothing save oblivion.

Everything was primitive — passion and pleasure ruled. To spend easily made money noisily, brazenly, was the ideal. From dawn to dawn the search after joy continued. The bagnios and dance halls were ablaze; the bar-rooms crowded with hilarious or quarrelsome humanity, the gambling tables alive with excitement. Men swaggered along the streets looking for trouble, and generally finding it; cowboys rode into open saloon doors and drank in the saddle; troops of congenial spirits, frenzied with liquor, spurred recklessly through the street firing into the air, or the crowd, as their whim led; bands played popular airs on balconies, and innumerable " barkers " added their honeyed invitations to the perpetual din. From end to end it was a saturnalia of vice, a babel of sound, a glimpse of the inferno. Money flowed like water; every man was his own law, and the gun the arbiter of destiny. The town marshal, with a few coolheaded deputies, moved here and there amid the chaos, patient, tireless, undaunted, seeking merely to exercise some slight restraint. This was Sheridan.

Into the one long street just at dusk rode Keith

and Neb, the third horse trailing behind. Already lights were beginning to gleam in the crowded saloons, and they were obliged to proceed slowly. Leaving the negro at the corral to find some purchaser for the animals, and such accommodations for himself as he could achieve, Keith shouldered his way on foot through the heterogeneous mass toward the only hotel, a long two-storied wooden structure, unpainted, fronting the glitter of the Pioneer Dance Hall opposite. A noisy band was splitting the air with discordant notes, a loud-voiced " barker " yelling through the uproar, but Keith, accustomed to similar scenes and sounds elsewhere, strode through the open door of the hotel, and guided by the noisy, continuous clatter of dishes, easily found his way to the dining-room. It was crowded with men, a few women scattered here and there, most of the former in shirt-sleeves, all eating silently. A few smaller tables at the back of the room were distinguished from the others by white coverings in place of oil-cloth, evidently reserved for the more distinguished guests. Disdaining ceremony, the newcomer wormed his way through, finally discovering a vacant seat where his back would be to the wall, thus enabling him to survey the entire apartment.

It was not of great interest, save for its constant change and the primitive manner in which the majority attacked their food supply, which was piled helter-skelter upon the long tables, yet he ran his eyes searchingly over the numerous faces, seeking impartially for either friend or enemy. No countenance present, as revealed in the dim light of the few swinging lamps, appeared familiar, and satisfied that he remained unknown, Keith began devoting his attention to the dishes before him, mentally expressing his opinion as to their attractiveness. Chancing finally to again lift his eyes, he met the gaze of a man sitting directly opposite, a man who somehow did not seem exactly in harmony with his surroundings. He was short and stockily built, with round rosy face, and a perfect shock of wiry hair brushed back from a broad forehead; his nose wide but stubby, and chin massive. Apparently he was between forty and fifty years of age, exceedingly well dressed, his gray eyes shrewd and full of a grim humor. Keith observed all this in a glance, becoming aware at the same time that his neighbor was apparently studying him also. The latter broke silence with a quick, jerky utterance, which seemed to peculiarly fit his personal appearance.

" Damn it all — know you, sir — sure I do — but for life of me can't tell where."

Keith stared across at him more searchingly, and replied, rather indifferently:

"Probably a mistake then, as I have no recollection of your face."

"Never make a mistake, sir — never forget a face," the other snapped with some show of indignation, his hands now clasped on the table, one stubby forefinger pointed, as he leaned forward. "Don't tell me — I 've seen you somewhere — no, not a word — don't even tell me your name — I 'm going to think of it."

Keith smiled, not unwilling to humor the man's eccentricity, and returned to his meal, with only an occasional inquiring glance across the table. The other sat and stared at him, his heavy eyebrows wrinkled, as he struggled to awaken memory. The younger man had begun on his pie when the face opposite suddenly cleared.

"Damn me, I 've got it — hell, yes; hospital tent — Shenandoah — bullet imbedded under third rib — ordinary case — that 's why I forgot — clear as mud now — get the name in a minute — Captain — Captain Keith — that 's it — shake hands."

Puzzled at the unexpected recognition, yet realizing the friendliness of the man, Keith grasped the pudgy fingers extended with some cordiality.

"Don't remember me I s'pose — don't think you ever saw me — delirious when I came — hate to tell you what you was talking about — gave you hypodermic first thing — behaved well enough though when I dug out the lead — Minié bullet, badly blunted hitting the rib — thought you might die with blood poison — could n't stay to see — too damn much to do — evidently did n't though — remember me now? "

" No, only from what you say.    You must have been at General Waite's headquarters."

" That 's it — charge of Stonewall's field hospital — just happened to ride into Waite's camp that night — damn lucky for you I did — young snip there wanted to saw the bone — I stopped that — liked your face — imagined you might be worth saving — ain't so sure of it now, or you would n't be out in this God forsaken country, eating such grub — my name 's Fairbain — Joseph Wright Fairbain, M.D.— contract surgeon for the railroad — working on the line? "

Keith shook his head, feeling awakening interest in his peculiar companion.

" No; just drifted in here from down on the Arkansas," he explained, briefly.  " Did you know General Waite was dead? "

The doctor's ruddy face whitened.

" Dead? — Willis Waite dead? " he repeated. " What do you mean, sir?  Are you sure?  When? "

" I ought to be sure; I buried him just this side the Cimmaron Crossing out on the Santa Fé trail."

"But do you know it was General Waite?" the man's insistent tone full of doubt.

"I have no question about it," returned Keith, conclusively. "The man was Waite's size and general appearance, with gray beard, similar to the one I remember he wore during the war. He had been scalped, and his face beaten beyond recognition, but papers in his pockets were sufficient to prove his identity. Besides, he and his companion — a young fellow named Sibley — were known to have pulled out two days before from Carson City."

"When was this?"

"Ten days ago."

Fairbain's lips smiled, the ruddy coloring sweeping back into his cheeks.

"Damn me, Keith, you came near giving me a shock," he said, jerkily. "Should n't be so careless — not sure my heart 's just right — tendency to apoplexy, too — got to be guarded against. Now, let me tell you something — maybe you buried some poor devil out at Cimmaron Crossing — but it was n't Willis Waite. How do I know? Because I saw him, and talked with him yesterday — damn me, if I did n't, right here in this town."

# CHAPTER XVII

## IN THE NEXT ROOM

K EITH, his eyes filled with undisguised doubt, studied the face of the man opposite, almost convinced that he was, in some way, connected with the puzzling mystery. But the honesty of the rugged face only added to his perplexity.

"Are you certain you are not mistaken?"

"Of course I am, Keith. I've known Waite for fifteen years a bit intimately — have met him frequently since the war — and I certainly talked with him. He told me enough to partially confirm your story. He said he had started for Santa Fé light, because he could n't get enough men to run a caravan — afraid of Indians, you know. So, he determined to take money — buy Mexican goods — and risk it himself. Old fighting cock would n't turn back for all the Indians on the plains once he got an idea in his head — he was that kind — Lord, you ought to seen the fight he put up at Spottsylvania! He got to Carson City with two wagons, a driver and a cook — had eight thousand dollars with him, too, the damn fool. Cook

148

got into row, gambling, cut a man, and was jugged.
Old Waite would n't leave even a nigger in that sort
of fix — natural fighter — likes any kind of row.   So,
he hung on there at Carson, but had sense enough —
Lord knows where he got it — to put all but a few
hundred dollars in Ben Levy's safe.   Then, he went
out one night to play poker with his driver and a
friend — had a drink or two — doped, probably, and
never woke up for forty-eight hours — lost clothes,
money, papers, and whole outfit — was just naturally
cleaned out — could n't get a trace worth following
after.   You ought to have heard him cuss when he told
me — it seemed to be the papers that bothered him
most — them, and the mules."

"You say there was no trace?"

"Nothing to travel on after forty-eight hours —
a posse started out next morning, soon as they found
him — when they got back they reported having run
the fellows as far as Cimmaron Crossing — there they
got across into the sand hills, and escaped."

"Who led the posse?"

"A man called Black, I think," he said.

"Black Bart?"

"Yes, that's the name; so, I reckon you did n't bury
Willis Waite this time, Captain.   You would n't
have thought he was a dead one if you had heard

him swear while he was telling the story — it did him proud; never heard him do better since the second day at Gettysburg — had his ear shot off then, and I had to fix him up — Lord, but he called me a few things."

Keith sat silent, fully convinced now that the doctor was telling the truth, yet more puzzled than ever over the peculiar situation in which he found himself involved.

"What brought the General up here?" he questioned, finally.

"I have n't much idea," was the reply. "I don't think I asked him directly. I was n't much interested. There was a hint dropped, however, now you speak about it. He 's keen after those papers, and does n't feel satisfied regarding the report of the posse. It 's my opinion he 's trailing after Black Bart."

The dining-room was thinning out, and they were about the only ones left at the tables. Keith stretched himself, looking around.

"Well, Doctor, I am very glad to have met you again, and to learn Waite is actually alive. This is a rather queer affair, but will have to work itself out. Anyway, I am too dead tired to-night to hunt after clues in midst of this babel. I 've been in the saddle most of the time for a week, and have got to find a bed."

"I reckon you won't discover such a thing here,"

dryly. " Got seven in a room upstairs, and others corded along the hall. Better share my cell — only thing to do."

" That would be asking too much — I can turn in at the corral with Neb; I 've slept in worse places."

" Could n't think of it, Keith," and the doctor got up. " Besides, you sleep at night, don't you? "

" Usually, yes," the other admitted.

" Then you won't bother me any — no doctor sleeps at night in Sheridan; that 's our harvest time. Come on, and I 'll show you the way. When morning comes I 'll rout you out and take my turn."

Keith had enjoyed considerable experience in frontier hotels, but nothing before had ever quite equalled this, the pride of Sheridan. The product of a mushroom town, which merely existed by grace of the temporary railway terminus, it had been hastily and flimsily constructed, so it could be transported elsewhere at a moment's notice. Every creak of a bed echoed from wall to wall. The thin partitions often failed to reach the ceiling by a foot or two, and the slightest noise aroused the entire floor. And there was noise of every conceivable kind, in plenty, from the blare of a band at the Pioneer Dance Hall opposite, to the energetic cursing of the cook in the rear. A discordant din of voices surged up from the street below — laughter, shouts, the shrieks of women, a rattle of dice, an occasional pistol shot, and the continuous yelling of industrious "barkers." There was no safety anywhere. An exploding revolver in No. 47 was quite likely to disturb the peaceful slumbers of the innocent occupant of No. 15, and every sound of quarrel in the thronged bar-room below caused the lodger to curl up in momentary expectation of a stray bullet coursing toward him through the floor. With this to trouble him, he could lie there and hear everything that occurred within and without. Every creak, stamp, and snore was faithfully reported; every curse, blow, snarl reëchoed to his ears. Inside was hell; outside was Sheridan.

Wearied, and half dead, as Keith was, sleep was simply impossible. He heard heavy feet tramping up and down the hall; once a drunken man endeavored vainly to open his door; not far away there was a scuffle, and the sound of a body falling down stairs. In some distant apartment a fellow was struggling to draw off his tight boots, skipping about on one foot amid much profanity. That the boot conquered was evident when the man crawled into the creaking bed, announcing defiantly, " If the landlord wants them boots off, let him come an' pull 'em off." Across the hall was a rattle of chips, and the voices of several men, occasionally raised in anger. Now and then they would stamp on

the floor as an order for liquid refreshments from below. From somewhere beyond, the long-drawn melancholy howl of a distressed dog greeted the rising moon.

Out from all this pandemonium Keith began to unconsciously detect the sound of voices talking in the room
to his left. In the lull of obstructing sound a few
words reached him through the slight open space between wall and ceiling.

"Hell, Bill, what's the use goin' out again when
we have n't the price?"

"Oh, we might find Bart somewhere, and he'd stake
us. I guess I know enough to make him loosen up.
Come on; I'm goin'."

"Not me; this town is too near Fort Hays; I'm
liable to run into some of the fellows."

A chair scraped across the floor as Bill arose to his
feet; evidently from the noise he had been drinking,
but Keith heard him lift the latch of the door.

"All right, Willoughby," he said, thickly, "I'll try
my luck, an' if I see Bart I'll tell him yer here. So
long."

He shuffled along the hall and went, half sliding,
down stairs, and Keith distinguished the click of glass
and bottle in the next room. He was sitting up in bed
now, wide awake, obsessed with a desire to investigate.
The reference overheard must have been to Hawley,

and if so, this Willoughby, who was afraid of meeting
soldiers from the fort, would be the deserter Miss Hope
was seeking. There could be no harm in making sure,
and he slipped into his clothes, and as silently as possible, unlatched his door. There was a noisy crowd
at the farther end of the hall, and the sound of some
one laboriously mounting the stairs. Not desiring to
be seen, Keith slipped swiftly toward the door of the
other room, and tried the latch. It was unfastened,
and he stepped quietly within, closing it behind him.

A small lamp was on the washstand, a half-emptied
bottle and two glasses beside it, while a pack of cards
lay scattered on the floor. Fully dressed, except for a
coat, the sole occupant lay on the bed, but started up
at Keith's unceremonious entrance, reaching for his
revolver, which had slipped to the wrong side of his
belt.

"What the hell!" he exclaimed, startled and confused.

The intruder took one glance at him through the
dingy light — a boy of eighteen, dark hair, dark eyes,
his face, already exhibiting signs of dissipation, yet
manly enough in chin and mouth — and smiled.

"I could draw while you were thinking about it,"
he said, easily, "but I am not here on the fight. Are
you Fred Willoughby?"

His was figure and face to be noted anywhere

The lad stared at him, his uncertain hand now closed on the butt of his revolver, yet held inactive by the other's quiet assurance.

" What do you want to know for? "

" Curiosity largely; thought I 'd like to ask you a question or two."

" You — you 're not from the fort? "

" Nothing to do with the army; this is a private affair."

The boy was sullen from drink, his eyes heavy.

" Then who the devil are you? I never saw you before."

" That 's very true, and my name would n't help any. Nevertheless, you 're perfectly welcome to it. I am Jack Keith." No expression of recognition came into the face of the other, and Keith added curtly, " Shall we talk? "

There was a moment's silence, and then Willoughby swung his feet over the edge of the bed onto the floor.

" Fire away," he said shortly, " until I see what the game is about."

## CHAPTER XVIII

### INTERVIEWING WILLOUGHBY

COOLLY, yet without in the least comprehending
how best to proceed, Keith drew toward him the
only chair in the room, and sat down.  Miss Hope —
more widely known as Christie Maclaire — had
claimed this drunken lad as her brother, but, according to Hawley, he had vehemently denied any such
relationship.  Yet there must be some previous association between the two, and what this was the plainsman
proposed to discover.  The problem was how best to
cause the fellow to talk frankly — could he be reached
more easily by reference to the girl or the gambler?
Keith studying the sullen, obstinate face confronting
him, with instinctive antagonism over his intrusion,
swiftly determined on the girl.

"It was not very nice of me to come in on you
this way," he began, apologetically, " but you see I happen to know your sister."

"My sister?  Oh, I guess not!"

"Yes, but I do," throwing a confidence into his tone

156

he was far from feeling, " Miss Hope and I are friends."

The boy sprang to his feet, his face flushed.

" Oh, you mean Hope? Do you know her? Say, I thought you were giving me that old gag about Christie Maclaire."

" Certainly not; who is she?"

" That's more than I know; fellow came to me at Carson, and said he'd met my sister on a stage west of Topeka. I knew he was lyin', because she's home over in Missouri. Finally, I got it out of him that she claimed to be my sister, but her name was Maclaire. Why, I don't even know her, and what do you suppose she ever picked me out for her brother for?"

He was plainly puzzled, and perfectly convinced it was all a mistake. That his sister might have left home since he did, and drifted West under an assumed name, apparently never occurred to him as possible. To Keith this was the explanation, and nothing could be more natural, considering her work, yet he did not feel like shattering the lad's loyalty. Faith in the sister might yet save him.

" Perhaps the fellow who told you," he hazarded blindly, speaking the first thought which came to his mind, " had some reason to desire to make you think this Maclaire girl was your sister."

The suggestion caused him to laugh at first; then his face suddenly sobered, as though a new thought had occurred to him.

" Damn me, no, it could n't be that," he exclaimed, one hand pressing his head. " He could n't be workin' no trick of that kind on me."

" Whom do you mean? "

" A fellow named Hawley," evasively. " The man who claimed to have met my sister."

" ' Black Bart ' Hawley? "

The boy lifted his head again, his eyes filled with suspicion.

" Yes, if you must know; he 's a gambler all right, but he 's stuck to me when I was down and out. You know him? "

" Just a little," carelessly; " but what sort of a trick could he be working trying to make you acknowledge Christie Maclaire as your sister? "

Willoughby did not answer, shifting uneasily about on the bed. Keith waited, and at last the boy blurted out:

" Oh, it was n't nothing much. I told him something when I was drunk once, that I thought maybe might have stuck to him. Odd he should make that mistake, too, for I showed him Hope's picture. Bart 's a schemer, and I did n't know but what he might have figured out a trick, though I don't see how he could.  It was n't no more than a pipe dream, I reckon.  Where did you meet Hope?  Back in Missouri?"

One thing was clearly evident — the boy's faith in his sister.  If he was to be rightly influenced, and led back to her, he must have no suspicion aroused that her life was any different from what it had been before he left home.  Besides if Keith hoped to gain any inkling of what Hawley's purpose could be, he must win the confidence of Willoughby.  This could not be done by telling him of Hope's present life.  These considerations flashed through his mind, and as swiftly determined his answer.

"Oh, I 've known her some time.  Not long ago I did her a service for which she is grateful.  Did you know she was out in this country searching for you?"

"Out here?  In Kansas?"

"Sure; that is n't much of a trip for a spirited girl.  She got it in her head from your letters that you were in trouble, and set out to find you and bring you home.  She did n't tell me this, but that is the way I heard it.  It was for her sake I came in here.  Why not go to her, Willoughby, and then both of you return to Missouri?"

The sullenness had gone out of the boy's face: he looked tired, discouraged.

" Where is Hope? " he asked.

" Fort Larned, I suppose.   She went to Carson City first."

" Well, that settles it," shaking his head.   " You don't suppose I could go browsin' 'round Larned, and not get snapped up, do you?   They don't chase deserters very far out here, but that's the post I skipped from, and they'd jug me all right.   Besides, I'm damned if I'll go back until I get a stake.   I want to see a fellow first."

" What fellow? "

" Well, it's Hawley, if you want to know so bad. He said if I would come here and wait for him he'd put me on to a good thing."

The boy fidgetted along the edge of the bed, evidently half ashamed of himself, yet obstinate and unyielding.   Keith sat watching his face, unable to evolve any means of changing his decision.   Hawley's influence just at present was greater than Hope's, because the lad naturally felt ashamed to go slinking home penniless and defeated.   His pride held him to Hawley, and his faith that the man would redeem his promise. Keith understood all this readily enough, and comprehended also that if " Black Bart " had any use for the boy it would be for some criminal purpose. What was it ? Was there a deeply laid plot back of all these preparations involving both Willoughby and his sister? What was it Hawley was scheming about so carefully, holding this boy deserter in one hand, while he reached out the other after Christie Maclaire? Surely, the man was not working blindly; he must have a purpose in view. Willoughby had acknowledged he had told the fellow something once when he was drunk — about his family history, no doubt, for he had shown him Hope's picture. What that family secret was Keith had no means of guessing, but Hawley, the moment he saw the face on the cardboard, had evidently recognized Christie Maclaire — had thought of some way in which what he now knew could be turned to advantage. The few scattered facts which Keith had collected all seemed to point to such a conclusion — Hawley had sent the boy to Sheridan, where he would be out of sight, with orders to wait for him there, and the promise of a " stake " to keep him quiet. Then he had gone to Independence and Topeka seeking after Christie Maclaire. Evidently he meant to keep the two apart until he had gained from each whatever it was he sought. But what could that be? What family secret could Willoughby have blurted out in his cups, which had so stimulated the gambler's wits?

Two things combined to cause Keith to determine he would uncover this rascality,— his desire to repay Hawley, and his interest in the girl rescued on the Salt Fork. This gossamer web of intrigue into which he had stumbled unwittingly was nothing to him personally; had it not involved both Hawley and Miss Hope, he would have left it unsolved without another thought. But under the circumstances it became his own battle. There was a crime here — hidden as yet, and probably not consummated — involving wrong, perhaps disgrace, to the young girl. He had rescued her once from out the clutches of this man, and he had no intention of deserting her now. Whatever her life might be, she was certainly an innocent victim in this case, deserving his protection. The memory came to him of her face upturned toward him in that little room of the Occidental, her eyes tear-dimmed, her lips asking him to come back to her again. He could not believe her a bad woman, and his lips compressed, his eyes darkened, with fixed determination. He would dig into this until he uncovered the truth; he would find out what dirty trick " Black Bart " was up to.

As he thought this out, not swiftly as recorded, but slowly, deliberately, piecing the bits together within his mind, blindly feeling his way to a final conclusion, the boy had sunk back upon the bed, overcome with liquor, and fallen asleep. Keith stepped over, and looked down upon him in the dim light. He could recognize something of her features in the upturned face, and his eyes softened. There was no use seeking again to arouse him; even had he been sober, he would not have talked freely. Keith lifted the dangling feet into a more comfortable position, turned the lamp lower, went out, and latched the door. Two men were tramping heavily up the stairs, and they turned into the hall at the very moment he disappeared within his own room. He still retained his grasp upon the latch, when a voice outside asked:

"What number did you say, Bill — 29?"

Keith straightened up as though suddenly pricked by a knife; he could never forget that voice — it was Hawley's.

# CHAPTER XIX

### A GLIMPSE AT CONSPIRACY

LEANING against the inside of his own door, startled by the rapid sequence of events, Keith was able, from different sounds reaching him, to mentally picture most of what occurred in the next room. He heard Bill sink down into the convenient chair, and drink from the bottle, while the gambler apparently advanced toward the bed, where he stood looking down on its unconscious occupant.

"The fool is dead drunk," he declared disgustedly. "We can't do anything with him to-night."

"I say — throw bucket water over him," hiccoughed the other genially, "allers sobers me off."

Hawley made no response, evidently finding a seat on one end of the washstand.

"Hardly worth while, Scott," he returned finally. "Perhaps I better have some understanding with Christie, anyhow, before I pump the boy any further. If we can once get her working with us, Willoughby won't have much hand in the play — we shan't need him. Thought I told you to keep sober?"

"Am sober," solemnly, "ain't had but six drinks; just nat'rly tired out."

"Oh, indeed; well, such a room as this would drive any man to drink.  Did you get what I sent you here after?"

"I sure did, Bart," and Keith heard the fellow get to his feet unsteadily.  "Here's the picture, an' some letters.  I did n't take only what he had in the grip."

Hawley shuffled the letters over in his hands, apparently hastily reading them with some difficulty in the dim light.

"Nothing there to give us any help," he acknowledged reluctantly, "mostly advice as far as I can see. Damn the light; a glow worm would be better." There was a pause; then he slapped his leg.  "However, it's clear they live in Springfield, Missouri, and this photograph is a peach.  Just look here, Bill! What did I tell you?  Ain't Christie a dead ringer for this girl?"

"You bet she is, Bart," admitted the other in maudlin admiration, "only, I reckon, maybe some older."

"Well, she ought to be accordin' to Willoughby's story, an' them papers bear him out all right, so I reckon he's told it straight — this Phyllis would be twenty-six now, and that's just about what Christie is.

It would n't have fit better if we had made it on purpose.   If the girl will only play up to the part we
won't need any other evidence — her face would be
enough."

Keith could hear the beating of his own heart in the
silence that followed.   Here was a new thought, a new
understanding, a complete new turn to affairs.   Christie
Maclaire, then, was not Willoughby's sister Hope.
The girl he rescued on the desert — the girl with the
pleading brown eyes, and the soft blur of the South
on her lips — was not the music hall singer.   He could
hardly grasp the truth at first, it antagonized so sharply
with all he had previously believed.   Yet, if this were
true his own duty became clearer than ever; aye, and
would be more willingly performed.   But what did
Hawley know?   Did he already realize that the girl
he had first met on the stage coach, and later inveigled
into the desert, was Hope, and not the music hall artist?
He, of course, fully believed her to be Christie Maclaire
at that time, but something might have occurred since
to change that belief.   Anyhow, the man was not now
seeking Hope, but the other.   Apparently the latter
was either already here in Sheridan or expected soon.
And exactly what was it the gambler desired this
Maclaire woman to do?   This was the important matter, and for its solution Keith possessed merely a few

hints, a few vague suggestions. She was expected to represent herself as Phyllis — Phyllis who? Some Phyllis surely whose physical resemblance to Hope must be sufficiently marked to be at once noticeable. Willoughby had evidently revealed to Hawley some hidden family secret, having money involved, no doubt, and in which the discovery of this mysterious Phyllis figured. She might, perhaps, be a sister, or half-sister, who had disappeared, and remained ignorant as to any inheritance. Hope's picture shown by the boy, and reminding Hawley at once of Christie Maclaire, had been the basis of the whole plot. Exactly what the details of that plot might be Keith could not figure out, but one thing was reasonably certain — it was proposed to defraud Hope. And who in the very truth was Hope? It suddenly occurred to him as a remarkably strange fact that he possessed not the slightest inkling as to the girl's name. Her brother had assumed to be called Willoughby when he enlisted in the army, and his companions continued to call him this. If he could interview the girl now for only five minutes he should be able probably to straighten out the whole intricate tangle. But where was she? Would she have remained until this time at Fort Larned with Kate Murphy?

There was a noise of movement in the next room.

Apparently as Hawley arose carelessly from his edge of the washstand he had dislodged the glass, which fell shivering on the floor. Scott swore audibly at the loss.

"Shut up, Bill," snapped the gambler, irritated, "you 've got the bottle left. I 'm going; there 's nothing for any of us to do now, until after I see Christie. You remain here! Do you understand? — remain here. Damn me, if that drunken fool is n't waking up."

There was a rattling of the rickety bed, and then the sound of Willoughby's voice, thick from liquor.

"Almighty glad see you, Bart — am, indeed. Want money — Bill an' I both want money — can't drink without money — can't eat without money — shay, when you goin' stake us?"

"I 'll see you again in the morning, Fred," returned the other briefly. "Go on back to sleep."

"Will when I git good an' ready — go sleep, stay wake, just as I please — don't care damn what yer do — got new frien' now."

"A new friend? Who?" Hawley spoke with aroused interest.

"Oh, he 's all right — he 's mighty fine fellow — come in wisout in — invitation — ol' friend my sister — called — called her Hope — you fool, Bart Hawley, think my sister Christie — Christie — damfino the name

— my sister, Hope — don't want yer money — my — my new friend, he 'll stake me — he knows my sister — Hope."

The gambler grasped the speaker, shaking him into some slight semblance of sobriety.

"Now, look here, Willoughby, I want the truth, and mean to have it," he insisted. "Has some one been in here while Scott was gone?"

"Sure — did n't I just tell yer? — friend o' Hope's."

"Who was he? Speak up! I want the name!"

There was a faint gurgling sound, as though the gambler's vise-like fingers were at the boy's throat; a slight struggle, and then the choked voice gasped out:

"Let up! damn yer! He called himself Jack Keith."

The dead silence which ensued was broken only by heavy breathing. Then Scott swore, bringing his fist down with a crash on the washstand.

"That rather stumps yer, don't it, Bart? Well, it don't me. I tell yer it 's just as I said from the first. It was Keith an' that nigger what jumped ye in the cabin. They was hidin' there when we rode in. He just nat'rly pumped the gal, an' now he 's up here trailin' you. Blame it all, it makes me laugh."

"I don't see what you see to laugh at. This Keith

is n't an easy man to play with, let me tell you. He
may have got on to our game."

"Oh, hell, Bart, don't lose your nerve. He can't
do anything, because we 've got the under holt. He 's
a fugitive; all we got to do is locate him, an' have
him flung back inter jail — there 's murder an' hoss-
stealing agin him."

Hawley seemed to be thinking swiftly, while his companion took another drink.

"Well, pard, ain't that so?"

"No, that trick won't work, Scott. We could do it
easily enough if we were down in Carson, where the boys
would help us out. The trouble up here is that 'Wild
Bill' Hickock is Marshal of Sheridan, and he and I
never did hitch. Besides, Keith was one of his deputies
down at Dodge two years ago — you remember when
Dutch Charlie's place was cleaned out? Well, Hickock
and Keith did that job all alone, and 'Wild Bill' is n't
going back on that kind of a pal, is he? I tell you
we 've got to fight this affair alone, and on the quiet.
Maybe the fellow don't know much yet, but he 's sure
on the trail, or else he would n't have been in here
talking to Willoughby. We 've got to get him, Scott,
somehow. Lord, man, there 's a clean million dollars
waiting for us in this deal, and I 'm ready to fight for
it. But I 'm damned sleepy, and I 'm going to bed.

You locate Keith to-morrow, and then, when you 're
sober, we 'll figure out how we can get to him best;
I 've got to set Christie right.    Good-night, Bill."

He went out into the hall and down the creaking
stairs, the man he wanted so badly listening to his de-
scending footsteps, half tempted to follow.    Scott did
not move, perhaps had already fallen drunkenly asleep
on his chair, and finally Keith crossed his own room,
and lay down.    The din outside continued unabated,
but the man's intense weariness overcame it all, and he
fell asleep, his last conscious thought a memory of
Hope.

# CHAPTER XX

### HOPE GOES TO SHERIDAN

THE discovery of the locket which had fallen from about Keith's neck made it impossible for Hope to remain quietly for very long in the hotel at Fort Larned. The more carefully she thought over the story of that murder at the Cimmaron Crossing, and Keith's tale of how he had discovered and buried the mutilated bodies, the more assured she became that that was where this locket came from, and that the slain freighter must have been her own father. She never once questioned the truth of Keith's report; there was that about the man which would not permit of her doubting him. He had simply failed to mention what he removed from the bodies, supposing this would be of no special interest.

Mrs. Murphy, hoping thus to quiet the apprehensions of her charge, set herself diligently at work to discover the facts. As her house was filled with transients, including occasional visitors from Carson City, and was also lounging headquarters for many of the officers from the near-by fort, she experienced no

difficulty in picking up all the floating rumors.    Out of
these, with Irish shrewdness, she soon managed to patch
together a consistent fabric of fact.

" Shure, honey, it 's not so bad the way they tell it
now," she explained, consolingly.    " Nobody belaves
now it was yer father that got kilt.    It was two fellers
what stole his outfit, clothes an' all, an' was drivin' off
wid 'em inter the sand hills.    Divil a wan does know
who kilt 'em, but there 's some ugly stories travellin'
about.    Some says Injuns; some says the posse run 'em
down; an' Black Bart an' his dirthy outfit, they swear it
was Keith.    Oi 've got me own notion.    Annyhow,
there 's 'bout three hundred dollars, some mules, an' a
lot o' valyble papers missin'."

" But if it was n't father, where is he now? "

" That 's what Oi 've been tryin' ter foind out.
First off he went out to the Cimmaron Crossing,
gyarded by a squad o' cavalry from the fort here.
Tommy Caine wint along, an' told me all about it.
They dug up the bodies, but niver a thing did they find
on 'em — not a paper, nor a dollar.    They 'd bin
robbed all roight.    The owld Gineral swore loike a wild
mon all the way back, Tommy said, an' the first thing
he did at Carson City was to start huntin' fer ' Black
Bart.'    He was two days gittin' on the trail av him;
then he heard the feller was gone away trapsing after

a singin' or dancin' gyurl called Christie Maclaire. She was supposed to be ayther at Topeky or Sheridan. A freighter told the owld man she was at Sheridan, an' so he started there overland, hopin' ter head off ' Black Bart.' Oi reckon we could a towld mor 'n that."

" What do you mean? "

" Why shure, honey, what 's the use tryin' ter decave me? Did n't Jack Keith, wid his own lips, tell me ye was Christie Maclaire? "

" But I 'm not! I 'm not, Mrs. Murphy. I don't even know the woman. It is such a strange thing; I cannot account for it — both those men mistook me for her, and — and I let them. I did n't care who the man Hawley supposed me to be, but I intended to have told Mr. Keith he was mistaken. I don't know why I did n't, only I supposed he finally understood. But I want you to believe, Mrs. Murphy — I am Hope Waite, and not Christie Maclaire."

" It 's little the loss to ye not ter be her, an' Oi 'm thinkin' loikely Jack Keith will be moighty well plased ter know the truth. What 's ' Black Bart ' so ayger ter git hold av this Maclaire gyurl fer? "

" I do not in the least know. He must have induced me to go to that place in the desert believing me to be the other woman. Yet he said nothing of any purpose; indeed, he found no opportunity."

Mrs. Murphy shook her head disparagingly.

"It was shure some divilment," she asserted, stoutly. "He 'll be up to some thrick wid the poor gyurl; Oi know the loikes av him.  Shure, the two av yez must look as much aloike as two payes in a pod.  Loikely now, it 's a twin sister ye 've got? "

Hope smiled, although her eyes were misty.

"Oh, no; Fred and I were the only children; but what shall I do?  What ought I to do? "

The Irish mouth of Kate Murphy set firmly, her blue eyes burning.

"It 's not sthrong Oi am on advisin'," she said, shortly, "but if it was me Oi 'd be fer foindin' out what all this mix-up was about.  There 's somethin' moighty quare in it.  It 's my notion that Hawley 's got hold av thim papers av yer father's.  The owld gint thinks so, too, an' that 's why he 's so hot afther catchin' him.  May the divil admoire me av Oi know where this Maclaire gyurl comes in, but Oi 'll bet the black divil has get her marked fer some part in the play.  What would Oi do?  Be goory, Oi 'd go to Sheridan, an' foind the Gineral, an' till him all I knew. Maybe he could piece it together, an' guess what Hawley was up ter."

Hope was already upon her feet, her puzzled face brightening.

" Oh, that is what I wanted to do, but I was not sure it would be best. How can I get there from here? "

" Ye 'd have ter take the stage back to Topeky; loikely they 'd be runnin' thrains out from there on the new road. It 'll be aisy fer me ter foind out from some av the lads down below."

The only equipment operating into Sheridan was a construction train, with an old battered passenger coach coupled to the rear. A squad of heavily armed infantrymen rode along, as protection against possible Indian raiders, but there was no crowd aboard on this special trip, as all construction work had been suspended on the line indefinitely, and most of the travel, there-fore, had changed to the eastward. The coach used had a partition run through it, and, as soon as the busy trainmen discovered ladies on board, they unceremo-niously drove the more bibulous passengers, protesting, into the forward compartment. This left Hope in comparative peace, her remaining neighbors quiet, taci-turn men, whom she looked at through the folds of her veil during the long, slow, exasperating journey, men-tally guessing at their various occupations. It was an exceedingly tedious, monotonous trip, the train slackening up, and jerking forward, apparently with-out slightest reason; then occasionally achieving a full stop, while men, always under guard, went ahead to fix up some bit of damaged track, across which the engineer dared not advance. At each bridge spanning the numerous small streams, trainmen examined the structure before venturing forward, and at each stop the wearied passengers grew more impatient and sarcastic, a perfect stream of fluent profanity being wafted back whenever the door between the two sections chanced to be left ajar.

Hope was not the only woman on board, yet a glance at the others was sufficient to decide their status, even had their freedom of manner and loud talking not made it equally obvious. Fearful lest she might be mistaken for one of the same class, she remained in silence, her veil merely lifted enough to enable her to peer out through the grimy window at the barren view slipping slowly past. This consisted of the bare prairie, brown and desolate, occasionally intersected by some small watercourse, the low hills rising and falling like waves to the far horizon. Few incidents broke the dead monotony; occasionally a herd of antelope appeared in the distance, silhouetted against the sky-line, and once they fairly crept for an hour through a mass of buffalo, grazing so close that a fusillade of guns sounded from the front end of the train. A little farther along she caught a glimpse of a troop of wild horses dashing recklessly down into a sheltering ravine. Yet principally all that

12

met her straining eyes was sterile desolation. Here and there a great ugly water tank reared its hideous shape beside the track, the engine always pausing for a fresh supply. Beside it was invariably a pile of coal, a few construction cars, a hut half buried under earth, loop-holed and barricaded, with several rough men loafing about, heavily armed and inquisitive. A few of these points had once been terminal, the surrounding scenery evidencing past glories by piles of tin cans, and all manner of debris, with occasionally a vacant shack, left deserted and forlorn.

Wearied and heartsick, Hope turned away from this outside dreariness to contemplate more closely her neighbors on board, but found them scarcely more interesting. Several were playing cards, others moodily staring out of the windows, while a few were laughing and talking with the girls, their conversation inane and punctuated with profanity. One man was figuring on a scratch pad, and Hope decided he must be an engineer employed on the line; others she classed as small merchants, saloon-keepers, and frontier riff-raff. They would glance curiously at her as they marched up and down the narrow aisle, but her veil, and averted face, prevented even the boldest from speaking. Once she addressed the conductor, and the man who was figuring turned and looked back at her, evidently attracted by the soft note of her voice. But he made no effort at advances, returning immediately to his pad, oblivious to all else.

It was growing dusk, the outside world, now consisting of level plains, fading into darkness, with a few great stars burning overhead. Trainsmen lit the few smoking oil lamps screwed against the sides of the car, and its occupants became little more than dim shadows. All by this time were fatigued into silence, and several were asleep, finding such small comfort as was possible on the cramped seats. Hope glanced toward the heretofore noisy group at the rear — the girl nearest her rested with unconscious head pillowed upon the shoulder of her man friend, and both were sleeping. How haggard and ghastly the woman's powdered face looked, with the light just above it, and all semblance of joy gone. It was as though a mask had been taken off. Out in the darkness the engine whistled sharply and then came to a bumping stop at some desert station. Through the black window a few lanterns could be seen flickering about, and there arose the sound of gruff voices speaking. The sleepers inside, aroused by the sharp stop, rolled over and swore, seeking easier postures. Then the front door opened, and slammed shut, and a new passenger entered. He came down the aisle, glancing carelessly at the upturned faces, and finally sank into the seat directly opposite Hope.   He was a broad shouldered man, his coat buttoned to the throat, with strong face showing clearly beneath the broad hat brim and lighted up with a pair of shrewd, kindly eyes. The conductor came through, nodded at him, and passed on.   Hope thought he must be some official of the road, and ventured to break the prolonged silence with a question:

"Could you tell me how long it will be before we reach Sheridan?"

She had partially pushed aside her veil in order to speak more clearly, and the man, turning at sound of her voice, took off his hat, his searching eyes quizzical.

"Well, no, I can't, madam," the words coming with a jerk.   "For I'm not at all sure we'll keep the track. Ought to make it in an hour, however, if everything goes right.   Live in Sheridan?"

She shook her head, uncertain how frankly to answer.

"No loss to you — worst place to live in on earth — no exceptions — I know — been there myself three months — got friends there likely?"

"I hardly know," she acknowledged doubtfully. "I think so, but I shall have to hunt some place in which to stay to-night.   Can you tell me of some — some respectable hotel, or boarding house?"

The man wheeled about, until he could look at her more clearly.

"That's a pretty hard commission, Miss," he returned uneasily: "There may be such a place in Sheridan, but I have never found it. Old Mother Shattuck keeps roomers, but she won't have a woman in the house. I reckon you'll have to try it at the hotel — I'll get you in there if I have to mesmerize the clerk — you'll find it a bit noisy though."

"Oh, I thank you so much. I don't mind the noise, so it is respectable."

He laughed, good humoredly.

"Well I don't propose to vouch for that — the proprietor ain't out there for his health — but, I reckon, you won't have no serious trouble — the boys mostly know a good woman when they see one — which isn't often — anyhow, they're liable to be decent enough as long as I vouch for you."

"But you know nothing of me."

"Don't need to — your face is enough — I'll get you the room all right."

She hesitated, then asked:

"Are you — are you connected with the railroad?"

"In a way, yes — I'm the contract surgeon — had to dig a bullet out of a water-tank tender back yonder

— fellow howled as though I was killing him — no nerve — mighty poor stuff most of the riff-raff out here — ball was n't in much below the skin — Indian must have plugged him from the top of the bluff — blame good shot too — ragged looking slug — like to see it? "

She shook her head energetically.

" Don't blame you — nothing very uncommon — get a dozen cases like it a day sometimes — stay in Sheridan, show you something worth while — very pretty surgical operation to-morrow — come round and get you if you care to see it — got to open the stomach — don't know what I 'll find — like to go? "

" Oh, no!  I 'm sure you mean it all kindly, but — but I would rather not."

" Hardly supposed you would — only knew one woman who cared for that sort of thing much — she was nursing for me during the war — had a hair lip and an eye like a dagger — good nurse though — rather have your kind round me — ever nurse any?  Could get you a dozen jobs in Sheridan — new prospects every night — fifty dollars a week — what do you say? "

" But I 'm not seeking work, Doctor," smiling in spite of her bewilderment.  " I have money enough with me."

" Well, I did n't know — thought maybe you wanted a job, and did n't like to ask for it — have known 'em

like that — no harm done — if you ever do want anything like that, just come to me — my name 's Fairbain — everybody knows me here — operated on most
of 'em — rest expect to be — Damn that engineer!
don't believe he knows whether he 's going ahead or
backing up." He peered out of the window, pressing
his face hard against the glass. " I reckon that 's Sheridan he 's whistling for now — don't be nervous — I 'll
see you make the hotel all right."

# CHAPTER XXI

## THE MARSHAL OF SHERIDAN

IT was called a depot merely through courtesy, consisting of a layer of cinders, scattered promiscuously so as to partially conceal the underlying mud, and a dismantled box car, in which presided ticket agent and telegrapher. A hundred yards below was the big shack where the railroad officials lodged. Across the tracks blazed invitingly the "First Chance" saloon. All intervening space was crowded with men, surging aimlessly about in the glare of a locomotive head light, and greeting the alighting passengers with free and easy badinage. Stranger or acquaintance made no difference, the welcome to Sheridan was noisily extended, while rough play and hoarse laughter characterized the mass.

Hope paused on the step, even as Dr. Fairbain grasped her hand, dinned by the medley of discordant sounds, and confused by the vociferous jam of humanity. A band came tooting down the street in a hack, a fellow, with a voice like a fog horn, howling on the front seat. The fellows at the side of the car surged aside to get a glimpse of this new attraction, and Fairbain, taking quick advantage of the opportunity thus presented, swung his charge to the cinders below. Bending before her, and butting his great shoulders into the surging crowd, he succeeded in pushing a passage through, thus finally bringing her forth to the edge of the street.

"Hey, there," he said shortly, grabbing a shirt-sleeved individual by the arm. "Where's Charlie?"

The fellow looked at him wonderingly.

"Charlie? Oh, you mean the 'Kid'? Well, he ain't here ter-night; had a weddin', an' is totin' the bridal couple 'round."

Fairbain swore discreetly under his breath, and cast an uncertain glance at the slender figure shrinking beside him. The streets of Sheridan were not over pleasant at night.

"Only hack in town is somewhere else, Miss," he explained briefly. "I reckon you and I will have to hoof it."

He felt the grip of her fingers on his sleeve.

"The boys are a little noisy, but it's just their way — don't mean anything — you hang on to me, an' keep the veil down — we'll be there in the shake of a dog's tail."

He helped her over the muddy crossing, and as they

reached a stretch of board walk, began expatiating on the various places lining the way.

"That's the 'Mammoth' over there,— dance hall back of it — biggest thing west of the Missouri — three men killed there last week — what for?   Oh, they got too fresh — that's the 'Casino,' and the one beyond is 'Pony Joe's Place '— cut his leg off since I 've been here — fight over a girl.   Ain't there any stores? — sure; they 're farther back — you see the saloons got in first — that's 'Sheeny Mike's' gambling joint you 're looking at — like to go over and see 'em play?   All right, just thought I 'd ask you — it 's early anyhow, and things would n't be goin' very lively yet.   Say, there, you red head, what are you trying to do? "

The fellow had lurched out of the crowd in such a manner as to brush partially aside the girl's veil, permitting the glare of " Sheeny Mike's " lights to fall full upon her revealed face.   It was accomplished so openly as to appear planned, but before he could reel away again, Fairbain struck out, and the man went down. With an oath he was on his feet, and Hope cowered back against her protector.   Each man had weapons drawn, the crowd scurrying madly to keep out of the line of fire, when, with a stride, a new figure stepped quietly in between them.   Straight as an arrow, broad shouldered, yet small waisted as a woman, his hair hanging low over his coat-collar, his face smooth shaven except for a long moustache, and emotionless, the revolvers in his belt untouched, he simply looked at the two, and then struck the revolver out of the drunken man's hand. It fell harmless to the ground.

"And don't you pick it up until I tell you, Scott," he said quietly. "If you do you 've got to fight me."

Without apparently giving the fellow another thought, he wheeled and faced the others.

"Oh, it 's you, is it, Doctor? The drunken fool won't make any more trouble. Where were you taking the lady?"

"To the hotel, Bill."

"I 'll walk along with you. I reckon the boys will give us plenty of room." He glanced over the crowd, and then more directly at Scott.

"Pick up your gun!" the brief words snapping out. "This is the second time I 've caught you hunting trouble. The next time you are going to find it. I saw you run into the lady — what did you do it for?"

"I only wanted to see who she was, Bill."

"You need n't call me Bill. I don't trot in your class. My name is Hickock to you. Was it any of your affair who she was?"

" I reckoned I know'd her, and I did."

The marshal turned his eyes toward Hope, and then back upon Scott, evidently slightly interested.

" So?  Recognized an old friend, I suppose?"

The slight sneer in " Wild Bill's " soft voice caused Scott to flame up in sudden passion.

" No, I did n't! but I called the turn just the same — she 's Christie Maclaire."

The marshal smiled.

" All right, little boy," he said soberly.  " Now you trot straight along to bed.  Don't let me catch you on the street again to-night, and I 'd advise you not to pull another gun — you 're too slow on the trigger for this town.  Come along, Doctor, and we 'll get Miss Maclaire to her hotel."

He shouldered his way through the collected crowd, the others following.  Hope endeavored to speak, to explain to Fairbain who she actually was, realizing then, for the first time, that she had not previously given him her name.  Amidst the incessant noise and confusion, the blaring of brass, and the jangle of voices, she found it impossible to make the man comprehend. She pressed closer to him, holding more tightly to his arm, stunned and confused by the fierce uproar.  The stranger steadily pushing ahead of them, and opening a path for their passage, fascinated her, and her eyes watched him curiously.  His name was an oddly familiar one, associated in vague memory with some of the most desperate deeds ever witnessed in the West, yet always found on the side of law and order; it was difficult to conceive that this quiet-spoken, mild-eyed, gently smiling man could indeed be the most famous gun fighter on the border, hated, feared, yet thoroughly respected, by every desperado between the Platte and the Canadian.  Beyond the glare and glitter of the Metropolitan Dance Hall the noisy crowd thinned away somewhat, and the marshal ventured to drop back beside Fairbain, yet vigilantly watched every approaching face.

"Town appears unusually lively to-night, Bill," observed the latter gravely, "and the boys have got an early start."

"West end graders just paid off," was the reply. "They have been whoopin' it up ever since noon, and are beginning to get ugly.  Now the rest of the outfit are showing up, and there will probably be something interesting happening before morning.  Would n't mind it so much if I had a single deputy worth his salt."

"What 's the matter with Bain?"

"Nothing, while he was on the job, but ' Red ' Haggerty got him in ' Pony Joe's ' shebang two hours ago; shot him in the back across the bar. Ned never even pulled his gun."

" I 'm sorry to hear that; what became of Haggerty ? "

The marshal let his eyes rest questioningly on the doctor's face for an instant.

" Well, I happened to be just behind Ned when he went in," he said gently, " and ' Red ' will be buried on ' Boots Hill ' to-morrow. I 'm afraid I don't give you much chance to show your skill, Doc," with a smile.

" If they all shot like you do, my profession would be useless. What 's the matter with your other deputies ? "

" Lack of nerve, principally, I reckon; ain't one of 'em worth the powder to blow him up. I 'd give something just now for a fellow I had down at Dodge — he was a man. Never had to tell him when to go in; good judgment too; was n't out hunting for trouble, but always ready enough to take his share. Old soldier in our army, Captain I heard, though he never talked much about himself; maybe you knew him — Jack Keith."

" Well, I reckon," in quick surprise, " and what 's more to the point, he 's here — slept in my room last night."

" Keith here? In Sheridan? And has n't even hunted me up yet? That 's like him, all right, but I honestly want to see the boy. Here 's your hotel. Shall you need me any longer? "

" Better step in with us, Bill," the doctor advised, " your moral influence might aid in procuring the lady a decent room."

" I reckon it might."

They passed together up the three rickety steps leading into the front hall, which latter opened directly into the cramped office; to the left was the wide-open barroom, clamorous and throbbing with life. A narrow bench stood against the wall, with a couple of half drunken men lounging upon it. The marshal routed them out with a single, expressive gesture.

" Wait here with the lady, Fairbain," he said shortly, " and I 'll arrange for the room."

They watched him glance in at the bar, vigilant and cautious, and then move directly across to the desk.

" Tommy," he said genially to the clerk. " I 've just escorted a lady here from the train — Miss Maclaire — and want you to give her the very best room in your old shebang."

The other looked at him doubtfully.

" Hell, Bill, I don't know how I 'm goin' to do that," he acknowledged. " She wrote in here to the boss for a room; said she 'd be along yesterday. Well, she did n't show up, an' so to-night we let a fellow have it. He 's up there now."

"Well, he 'll have to vamose — who is he?"

"Englishman —'Walter Spotteswood Montgomery,' " consulting his book. "Hell of a pompous duck; the boys call him ' Juke Montgomery.' "

"All right; send some one up to rout his lordship out lively."

Tommy shuffled his feet, and looked again at the marshal; he had received positive orders about that room, and was fully convinced that Montgomery would not take kindly to eviction. But Hickock's quiet gray eyes were insistent.

"Here, ' Red,' " he finally called to the burly porter, "hustle up to ' 15,' an' tell that fellow Montgomery he 's got to get out; tell him we want the room for a lady."

Hickock watched the man disappear up the stairs, helped himself carefully to a cigar out of the stand, tossing a coin to the clerk and then deliberately lighting up.

"Think Montgomery will be pleased?" he asked shortly.

"No; he 'll probably throw ' Red ' down stairs."

The marshal smiled, his glance turning expectantly in that direction.

"Then perhaps I had better remain, Tommy." And he strolled nonchalantly over to the open window, and stood there looking quietly out, a spiral of blue smoke rising from his cigar.

They could distinctly hear the pounding on the door above, and occasionally the sound of the porter's voice, but the straight, erect figure at the window remained motionless.    Finally " Red " came down, nursing his knuckles.

" Says he 'll be damned if he will — says he 's gone to bed, an' that there ain't a cussed female in this blasted country he 'd git up for," he reported circumstantially to the clerk.    " He told me to tell you to go plumb to hell, an' that if any one else come poundin' 'round thar to-night, he 'd take a pot shot at 'em through the door.  ' Fifteen ' seemed a bit peevish, sir, an' I reckoned if he was riled up much more, he might git rambunctious; his language was sure fierce."

" Wild Bill " turned slowly around, still calmly smoking, his eyes exhibiting mild amusement.

" Did you clearly inform Mr.— ah — Montgomery that we desired the room for the use of a lady ? " he questioned gently, apparently both pained and shocked.

13

"I did, sir."

"It surprises me to find one in our city with so little regard for the ordinary courtesies of life, Tommy. Perhaps I can persuade the gentleman."

He disappeared up the stairs, taking them deliberately step by step, the cigar still smoking between his lips. "Red" called after him.

"Keep away from in front of the door, Bill; he 'll shoot sure, for he cocked his gun when I was up there."

Hickock glanced back, and waved his hand.

"Don't worry — the room occupied by Mr.— ah — Montgomery was ' 15,' I believe you said? "

Whatever occurred above, it was over with very shortly. Those listening at the foot of the stairs heard the first gentle rap on the door, an outburst of profanity, followed almost instantly by a sharp snap, as if a lock had given way, then brief scuffling mingled with the loud creaking of a bed. Scarcely a minute later the marshal appeared on the landing above, one hand firmly gripped in the neck-band of an undershirt, thus securely holding the writhing, helpless figure of a man, who swore violently every time he could catch his breath.

"Any other room you could conveniently assign Mr. — ah — Montgomery to, Tommy? " he asked pleasantly.   " If he does n't like it in the morning, he could be changed, you know."

" Give — give him ' 47.' "

" All right.   I 'm the bell-boy temporarily, Montgomery; easy now, my man, easy, or I 'll be compelled to use both hands.   ' Red,' carry the gentleman's luggage to ' 47 '— he has kindly consented to give up his old room to a lady — come along, Montgomery."

It was possibly five minutes later when he came down, still smoking, his face not even flushed.

" Montgomery is feeling so badly we were obliged to lock him in," he reported to the clerk.   " Seems to be of a somewhat nervous disposition.   Well, good-night, Doctor," he lifted his hat.   " And to you, Miss, pleasant dreams."

Hope watched him as he stepped outside, pausing a moment in the shadows to glance keenly up and down the long street before venturing down the steps.   This quiet man had enemies, hundreds of them, desperate and reckless; ceaseless vigilance alone protected him. Yet her eyes only, and not her thoughts, were riveted on the disappearing marshal.   She turned to Fairbain, who had risen to his feet.

" I wish I might see him, also," she said, as though continuing an interrupted conversation.

" See him?   Who? "

" Mr. Keith.   I — I knew him once, and — and,
Doctor, won't you tell him I should like to have him
come and see me just — just as soon as he can."

# CHAPTER XXII

AN INTERRUPTED INTERVIEW

MISS CHRISTIE MACLAIRE, attired in a soft lounging robe, her luxuriant hair wound simply about her head, forming a decidedly attractive picture, gazed with manifest dissatisfaction on the bare walls of her room, and then out through the open window into the comparatively quiet street below. The bar-tender at the " Palace," directly opposite, business being slack, was leaning negligently in the doorway. His roving eyes caught the fair face framed in the window, and he waved his hand encouragingly. Miss Christie's big brown eyes stared across at him in silent disgust, and then wandered again about the room, her foot tapping nervously on the rag carpet.

" It 's my very last trip to this town," she said decisively, her red lips pressed tightly together.

Miss Maclaire had indeed ample reason to feel aggrieved over her reception. She had written to have the best apartment in the house reserved for her, and then, merely because she had later been invited out to Fort Hays, and was consequently a day behind in arrival, had discovered that another woman — a base imposter, actually masquerading under her name — had been duly installed in the coveted apartment. Driving in from the fort that morning, accompanied by two of the more susceptible junior officers, conscious that she had performed most artistic work the evening before in the spacious mess-hall, and feeling confident of comfortable quarters awaiting her, it had been something of a shock to be informed by the perturbed clerk that " 15 " was already occupied by another. " A lady what come in last night, and I naturally supposed it was you."

In vain Miss Maclaire protested, ably backed by the worshipful officers who still gallantly attended her; the management was obdurate. Then she would go up herself, and throw the hussy out. Indeed, too angry for bantering further words, Christie had actually started for the stairs, intending to execute her threat, when the perspiring Tommy succeeded in stopping her, by plainly blurting out the exact truth.

" Don't you ever do it," he insisted. " The marshal brought her in here, and fired a fellow out o' the room so as to give it to her. He'd clean out this house if we ran in a cold deck on a friend o' his."

" What do I care for what your marshal does? "

" But he 's Bill Hickock, Miss, ' Wild Bill.' "

Miss Maclaire leaned back against the stair-rail, her eyes turning from Tommy to her speechless supporters. Slowly the truth seemed to penetrate her brain.

" Oh," she gasped at last. " Then — then what else can you give me? "

The officers had long since departed, promising, however, to remain over in town and hear her again that night at the Trocadero, with hints as to a late supper; she had received a call from the manager of that most popular resort, and had rendered his life miserable by numerous demands; had passed half an hour practising with the leader of the orchestra; but now was at last alone, tired, decidedly irritable, and still tempted to invade " 15," and give that other woman a piece of her mind. Then someone rapped on the door. There was a decided accent of vexation in the voice which bade the one outside enter, but the lady's mood changed swiftly as her brown eyes perceived standing in the doorway the erect form of Keith, the light from the window revealing clearly his strong face. The man stood hat in hand, bowing slightly, unable to comprehend why he should have been sent for, yet marvelling again at the remarkable resemblance between this woman and

that other whom he had left at Fort Larned.   As Miss
Maclaire stood with back toward the window, she presented the same youthful appearance, the same slenderness of figure, the same contour of face.

" Miss Christie Maclaire? " he asked, as though in
doubt.

" Yes," graciously, won instantly by the man's appearance and manner, " you wished to see me?   Will
you be seated? "

He crossed the narrow room to the stiff-backed chair
indicated, and the lady sank negligently down into her
own, resting her head against a pillow, and regarding
him expectantly.   He could view her now much more
distinctly, observing the slight difference in age, the
fuller lips, the darker shade of the hair, and the varied
expression of the eyes.   It was as if a different soul
looked forth from the same face.   He had never before realized how little, apparently trifling, details
marked the human countenance, and, embarrassed by
her own scrutiny, his glance swept about the room.
Misunderstanding this shifting of eyes, Miss Christie
sought to place the man more at ease.

" The room is a perfect fright," she observed
briskly, " but what can one expect in these mushroom
towns?   Really I had never been here before, or I
should n't have come.   They pay good money though

for talent, and we all have to live, you know.    Are —
are you in professional work? "

He shook his head, smiling, somewhat perplexed at
his reception.

" Really I didn't suppose you were," she went on,
" you don't look it.    But there are so many who come
to me to help them, that I have grown suspicious of
every stranger.    May I ask why you desired to see
me? "

Another suspicion had taken possession of her mind,
for the men of that section were never backward in
exhibiting admiration, yet somehow this man did not
seem exactly of that kind.

" I came merely because I was sent for, Miss
Maclaire," he replied, his gray eyes once again upon
her face.    " Doctor Fairbain gave me your message;
I am Jack Keith."

She looked the complete astonishment she felt, sitting
up in the chair, her eyes filled with questioning doubt.

" Doctor Fairbain!    My message!    Surely you are
mistaken?    I know no one of that name, and have sent
no message."

" You did not express a desire to see me? "

She laughed, exhibiting a row of white teeth.

" Certainly not; not until this moment was I even
aware of the existence of Mr. Jack Keith."

His own eyes smiled in response to the challenge of hers.

"I can assure you the surprise was mine also," he hastened to inform her, now more at ease, as he grasped the situation. "I could not understand how I had become known to you, yet I pledge you my word the message was actually brought. Of course you may suspicion otherwise, for I have seen you on the stage, and being a normal man, have wished that I could devise some excuse for meeting you."

"Indeed!" her eye-brows slightly uplifted.

"Yes, I make that confession frankly, yet this call comes from no such desire. I had no question when I came, but what I had been sent for — you will believe this?"

"I suppose I must, yet it seems very peculiar," she replied, feeling convinced that he was a gentleman, and troubled as to what she had best do. "Yet now that you have discovered your mistake —"

"I hope to take advantage of the opportunity," he broke in firmly, leaning slightly forward. "May I ask you a question?"

"I could hardly prevent it, and really I do not know that I have anything to conceal."

"Then I will risk the effort — do you know a man named Hawley? — Bartlett Hawley?"

Her eyes did not falter, although a red spot shot into her cheeks, and her lips pressed together.

"No; that is I have never met him," she acknowledged, just a trifle confused. " But I have received two letters signed by that name, and rather expected the gentleman would call upon me here in Sheridan during my engagement. Is that your mission? Were you sent by him? or are you Mr. Hawley?"

" I disclaim all relation, Miss Maclaire, even friendship. You, of course, know who this individual is?"

" No," the short monosyllable was not encouraging. " His messages were of a business character."

" So I presumed, yet one likes to know something even of the person he does business with. I have been acquainted with Hawley for several years, and have never been aware of any honorable business he has ever engaged in. He is a professional gambler, known on the frontier as ' Black Bart '; last night he was running a faro game across there in the ' Palace.' I cannot help wondering what kind of business such a fellow could possibly have with you, Miss Maclaire."

The woman's eyes flashed, hardening in their brown depths.

" What right have you to ask?" she began indignantly. " I am capable of deciding my own affairs. As I have told you I have never met Mr. Hawley, but I am not to be influenced against him merely by the denunciation of an avowed enemy. He has written me of something he has discovered which is of deep personal interest to me, and has promised to tell me the details, as well as place within my hands certain necessary papers."

"I appreciate your feelings," he said gently, as she paused, "but would you mind telling me the nature of those papers?"

There was something in Keith's face which told of honesty, and inspired confidence. Miss Maclaire's worldly experience had given her deep insight into the character of men, and somehow, as she looked into the clear gray eyes, she felt impelled to answer, a vague doubt of the unknown Hawley in her mind.

"They — they were papers to establish identity. He had discovered them by accident; they have to do with an inheritance. Really that is all I know, for he wrote very briefly, stating it would be safer to confer with me personally — only I imagine there is a large sum involved."

"From whose estate?"

"My grandfather's."

"And his name was?"

"Why — why, Mr. Keith, actually I do not know. It may seem strange, but — but I cannot even tell the names of my parents; I cannot remember either my father or mother. Oh, I do not know why I should tell you all this! Who are you, really? Why do you ask me such questions?"

He leaned forward, touched by the woman's emotion.

"Miss Maclaire," he said gravely. "I am not prying into your life needlessly, but am endeavoring to serve you as well as others. Hawley may indeed possess papers of great value, but if so they were not found by accident, but stolen from the body of a murdered man. These papers may possibly refer to you, but if so Hawley himself does not believe it — he has simply chosen you to impersonate the right party because of your physical resemblance."

"Resemblance to whom?"

"To a young woman, a Miss Hope."

"But how do you know this? Why should you be interested? Are you a detective?"

"No, I am not a detective, but I cannot explain to you my interest. I am trying to serve you, to keep you from being drawn into a plot —"

"Rather to keep me from learning the truth, Mr. Jack Keith," she burst forth, rising to her feet indignantly. "You are here trying to prejudice me against Mr. Hawley. He is your enemy, and you have come to me stabbing him in the back for revenge. That is your interest. Well, I am going to see the man, and consider what he has to say. I don't care half so much about the money as I do to find out who I am. If he can throw any light on my early life, on my parentage, I shall be the happiest woman in the world. I am sorry I told you anything — but I am going to see him just the same. Perhaps he might tell me something about you."

They were both standing, the woman's eyes flashing angrily, defiantly, her hands clinched. Keith, realizing the false position into which he had drifted, hesitated to answer. He meant to tell her the whole story, and urge her to coöperate with him in learning the gambler's purpose. The woman impressed him as honest at heart, in spite of her life and environment; she was not one whom a swindler could easily dupe into becoming a tool.

"Miss Maclaire," he began, determined on his course, "listen to me for just a moment. I am —"

There was a rap at the door. The eyes of both turned that way, and then Keith backed slowly into the darkened corner beyond the window, his right hand thrust into the pocket of his coat. Miss Maclaire observed the movement, her lips smiling, a red flush on either cheek. Then she stepped across the room, and

opened the door. Framed against the black background of the hall, his dark, rather handsome face
clearly revealed as he fronted the window, his black,
audacious eyes fixed appreciatively upon the lady, stood
" Black Bart " Hawley. He saw no one but her,
realized no other presence, had no thought except to
make a good impression. He was facing a beautiful
woman, whom he sought to use, and he bowed low, hat
in hand.

" Miss Maclaire," he said, pleasantly, " I trust you
will pardon all that has occurred between us, and permit me to explain."

" I — I do not understand," she replied, puzzled
by these unexpected words. " There has nothing occurred between us, I am sure, which requires explanation. Have we met before? "

The man smiled. Seeing the woman's face in the
shadows he was still convinced she was the same
he had last parted with on the Salt Fork. However,
if she preferred to ignore all that, and begin their re-
lations anew, it was greatly to his liking. It gave him
insight into her character, and fresh confidence that he
could gain her assistance. Anyhow, he was ready
enough to play her game.

" Let us assume not," just the slightest trace of
mockery in the tone, " and begin anew. At least, you

will confess the receipt of my letters — I am Bartlett Hawley."

She cast a half-frightened glance toward Keith, and the man, following the direction of her eyes, perceived the presence of the other. His right leg went backward, his hand dropping to the belt, his form stiffening erect. Keith's voice, low but clear in the silence, seemed to cut the air.

" Not a motion, Hawley!  I have you covered."

" Oh, gentlemen, please don't ! "

" Have no fear, Miss Maclaire; this man and I will settle our differences elsewhere, and not in your presence." He stepped forth into the middle of the room, revolver drawn, but held low at the hip, his watchful eyes never deserting the gambler's face.

" Back up against the wall, Hawley," he commanded. " I hardly need to tell you how I shoot, for we, at least, have met before.  Now, I 'm going out, and leave you to your interview with Miss Maclaire, and I wish you happiness and success."

He moved across to the opening, keeping his face toward his adversary; then backed out slowly, closed the door with a snap, and sprang aside to avoid any possibility of a bullet crashing after him. No sound of movement from within reached his ears, however, and he walked silently to the head of the stairs.

# CHAPTER XXIII

## AN UNEXPECTED MEETING

KEITH paused at the landing, looking down into the deserted office, almost tempted to return and force Hawley into a confession of his purpose. It was easy for him to conceive what would be the final result of this interview between the artistic gambler and Miss Maclaire. In spite of the vague suspicion of evil which the plainsman had implanted within the woman's mind, the other possessed the advantage, and would certainly improve it. All conditions were decidedly in his favor. He merely needed to convince the girl that she was actually the party sought, and she would go forward, playing the game he desired, believing herself right, totally unconscious of any fraud. The very simplicity of it rendered the plot the more dangerous, the more difficult to expose. Hawley had surely been favored by fortune in discovering this singer who chanced to resemble Hope so remarkably, and who, at the same time, was in such ignorance as to her own parentage. She would be ready to grasp at a straw, and, once persuaded

14                          209

as to her identity and legal rights, could henceforth be trusted implicitly as an ally.

Realizing all this, and comprehending also how easily Hawley would win her confidence and overcome his warning by denouncing him as a fugitive from justice charged with murder, the temptation to return and fight it out then and there became almost overpowering. He had no fear of Hawley; indeed, physical fear had scarcely a place in his composition, but he was not as yet sufficiently fortified with facts for the seeking of such an encounter. He could merely guess at the truth, unable to produce any proof with which to meet the gambler's certain denial.

A man came in through the office, and began climbing the stairs. He was almost at the landing before Keith recognized him or the other glanced up.

"Ah — seen her, I suppose?"

"Yes," returned Keith, not thinking it worth while to mention the lady's denial of having sent for him. "I have just come from there."

"Hum — thought you 'd be through by this time — fine looking girl, ain't she? — believe I 'll run in and chat with her myself."

"I would advise you to select some other time, Doctor," said the younger, drily, "as the lady has a visitor at present."

"A visitor?" his face rosy, his shrewd eyes darkening. "Ah, indeed! Of the male sex?"

"I judge so — 'Black Bart' Hawley."

"Good Lord!" so startled his voice broke. "Did he see you?"

"Rather; I backed him up against the wall with a gun while I made my adieu."

"But what brought him there? Are they acquainted?"

"Don't ask conundrums, Doctor. He may be your rival with the fair lady for all I know. If he is, my sympathies are all with you. Only I would n't try to see Miss Christie just now; I 'd wait for a clearer field. Hawley is probably not in the best of humor."

Fairbain stared into the face of the speaker, uncertain whether or not he was being laughed at.

"Reckon you 're right," he acknowledged at last. "Tired, anyhow — been out all night — thought I 'd like to see her again, though — finest looking woman I 've met since I came West — remarkable eyes — well, I 'll go along to bed — see you again to-morrow, Jack."

Keith watched the sturdy figure stomp heavily down the hall-way, loose boards creaking under his positive tread, and smiled to himself at the thought that he might have, indeed, become truly interested in the music hall singer. Somehow, the doctor did not harmonize with the conception of love, or fit graciously into the picture. Still, stranger matings had occurred, and Cupid does not ask permission before he plays pranks with hearts. Keith turned again toward the stairs, only to observe a woman slowly cross the office and commence the ascent. She was in the shadow, her face even more deeply shaded by her hat, yet he stared at her in amazement — surely, it was Miss Maclaire! Yet how could it be? He had left that person scarcely five minutes before in " 26," and this stairway was the only exit. His hand grasped the rail, his heart throbbing strangely, as a suspicion of the truth crossed his brain. Could this be Hope? Could it be that she was here also? As her foot touched the landing, she saw him, her eyes lighting up suddenly in recognition, a wave of color flooding her cheeks.

" Why, Captain Keith," she exclaimed, extending her gloved hand frankly, " you have been to my room, and were going away. I am so glad I came in time."

" I hardly thought to meet you," he replied, retaining her fingers in his grasp. " When did you reach Sheridan ? "

" Only last night. I had no idea you were here, until Doctor Fairbain chanced to mention your name. Then I at once begged him to tell you how exceedingly anxious I was to see you. You see, I was sure you

would come if you only knew.  I really thought you
would be here this morning, and remained in my room
waiting, but there were some things I actually had to
have.  I was n't out ten minutes, so you must n't think
I sent you a message and then forgot."

The nature of the mistake was becoming apparent,
and Keith's gray eyes smiled as they looked into the
depths of the brown.

"Your message had rather an amusing result," he
said, "as the doctor informed me that Miss Christie
Maclaire was the one who desired my presence."

"Miss Maclaire!" her voice exhibiting startled surprise.  "Why — why — oh, I did forget; I never told
him differently.  Why, it was most ridiculous."  She
laughed, white teeth gleaming between the parted red
lips, yet not altogether happily.  "Let me explain,
Captain Keith, for really I have not been masquerading.
Doctor Fairbain and I arrived upon the same train
last evening.  He is such a funny man, but was very
nice, and offered to escort me to the hotel.  I remember
now that although he introduced himself, I never
once thought to mention to him my name.  The town
was very rough last night — the company had paid off
the graders I was told — and there was no carriage, so
we were compelled to walk.  I — I never saw such a
mob of drunken men.  One came reeling against me,

and brushed aside my veil so as to see my face. The doctor struck him, and then the marshal came up — you know him, Bill Hickock — and the impudent fellow actually declared he knew me, that I was Christie Maclaire. I tried to explain, but they hurried me on through the crowd to the hotel, and I became confused, and forgot. Do you suppose they registered me by that name?"

"Quite likely; at least Fairbain still believes it was the fair Christie whom he so gallantly escorted last night."

"How provoking," her foot tapping the floor, a little wrinkle between her eyes. "It seems as though I couldn't escape that woman — does she — does she really look like me?"

"At a little distance, yes," he admitted, "her form and face resemble yours very closely, but her hair is darker, her eyes have a different expression, and she must be five or six years older."

"Do — do you know her well?"

"No, indeed; I have seen her several times on the stage, but never met her until a few moments ago."

"A few moments ago! Do you mean she is here in this hotel?"

"Yes, Miss Hope, and that was what made the mistake in names so laughable. Fairbain gave me your message, but as coming from Christie. I was, of course, greatly surprised, yet responded. The lady very promptly denied having sent for me, but as I was anxious to interview her myself, we managed to drift into conversation, and I must have passed a half hour there. I might have been there still, but for an interruption."

" Oh, indeed! " with rising inflection.

He glanced quickly about, reminded of the situation.

" Yes, Hawley came in, and I would prefer not to meet him here, or have him discover you were in Sheridan. Could we not go to your room? I have much to tell you."

Her questioning eyes left his face, and stared down over the rail. A heavily built man, with red moustache, leaned against the clerk's desk, his face toward them.

" Do you know that man? " she asked quickly. " He followed me all the time I was shopping. I — I believe he is the same one who jostled me in the crowd last night."

Keith leaned past her to get a better view, but the fellow turned, and slouched away.

" I only had a glimpse, but have no recollection of ever seeing him before. You heard no name? "

" ' Wild Bill ' called him either Scott, or Scotty —
if this is the same man."

Keith's jaw set, the fighting light burning in his eyes.
That was the name of the fellow rooming with Willoughby, the one who seemed to be Hawley's special
assistant.    Was he here as a spy?    His hands clinched
on the rail.    He was anxious to go down and wring the
truth out of him, but instead, he compelled his eyes to
smile, turning back to the girl.

" A mere accident probably; but about my request?
May I talk with you a few moments alone? "

She bowed, apparently still dissatisfied regarding his
lengthy conversation with Christie, yet permitted him
to follow down the hall.    She held open the door of
" 15," and he entered silently, not wholly understanding
the change in her manner.    She stood before the
dresser, drawing off her gloves and removing her hat.

" Will you be seated, Captain; the arm-chair by the
window is the more comfortable."    She turned toward
him, almost shyly, yet with womanly curiosity which
would not be stilled.    " Was your call upon Miss
Maclaire very interesting?    Did you admire her very
much? "

Keith's eyes lifted to her face, his ears quick to detect the undertone in her voice.

" Interesting? yes, for I was seeking after information, and met with some success.    As to the other question, I am not sure whether I admire the lady or not. She is bright, pretty, and companionable, and in spite of her profession, at heart, I believe, a good woman. But really, Miss Hope, I was too deeply immersed in my purpose to give her personality much consideration.    Among other things we spoke of you."

" Of me?   Why? "

" I told her something of our adventures together; of how both Hawley and I had been confused.   She was anxious to learn who you were, but unfortunately, I have never, even yet, heard your name."

" You have not? "

" No; I left you at Fort Larned believing you Christie Maclaire — supposing it your stage name, of course — and was confirmed in this belief by finding in the holster of the saddle you had been riding an envelope bearing that address."

" I remember; it contained the note the man brought to me from Hawley; he had written it that way."   She crossed the room, sinking down into a chair facing him. " And you have actually confused me with Christie Maclaire all this while?   Have never known who I was? "

He shook his head.

"I told you to call me Hope; that is my name — I am Hope Waite."

"Waite!" he leaned forward, startled by the possibility —"not — not —"

"Yes," she burst in, holding out her hands, clasping the locket, "and this was my father's; where did you get it?"

He took the trinket from her, turning it over in his fingers. Little by little the threads of mystery were being unravelled, yet, even now, he could not see very far. He looked up from the locket into her questioning face.

"Did I not tell you? No; then it was an oversight. This was about the throat of one of the men I buried at Cimmaron Crossing, but — but, Hope, it was not your father."

"I know," her voice choking slightly. "Mrs. Murphy found that out; that is why I am here. I heard my father came to Sheridan, and I wanted you to help me find him."

He was thinking, and did not answer at once, and she went on in some alarm.

"Do you know anything about him, Captain Keith? Where is he? Why is he here? Don't be afraid to tell me."

He pressed the locket back into her hand, retaining the latter, unresisted, within his own.

" I have not seen your father, Hope, but he was certainly here a few days ago, for Fairbain met him. They were together in the army.  I am going to tell you all I know — it seems to be a tangled web, but the ends must be somewhere, although, I confess, I am all at sea."

He told it slowly and simply, bringing forth his earlier suspicion, and how he had stumbled upon facts apparently confirming them.  He related her father's robbery, his loss of valuable papers, and the conversation between Hawley and Scott which led to the suspicion that these same papers had fallen into the hands of the former, and were the basis of his plot. Hope listened, breathless with interest, her widely opened eyes filled with wonder.  As he concluded speaking she burst forth:

" But I don't understand in the least, Captain Keith. Why did this man Hawley send me to the Salt Fork ? "

" He thought he was dealing with Christie Maclaire. He had some reason for getting her away; getting her where he could exercise influence over her."

" Yes — yes; but who is she ? "

" That is what makes the matter so hard to unravel. She does n't even know herself.  Hawley is going to take advantage of her ignorance in this respect, and convince her that she is the person he wishes her to represent — but who is the person? If we knew that we might block the game."

Both sat silent, striving to figure out some reasonable explanation.

" Do you know of any special papers your father carried? " he asked.

" No; none outside his business agreements."

" Has anyone ever disappeared connected with your family? Did you have an older sister? "

" Fred and I were the only children. Why should you ask that question? " .

" Because something of that nature would seem to be the only rational explanation. Your brother must have told Hawley something — some family secret — which he felt could be utilized to his own advantage. Then he saw your picture, and was immediately reminded of the remarkable resemblance between you and Christie Maclaire. Evidently this discovery fitted into his plan, and made it possible for him to proceed. He has been trying ever since to get an interview with the woman, to sound her, and find out what he can do with her. He has written letters, sufficiently explicit to make it clear his scheme is based upon a will drawn, as he claims, by Christie's grandfather. No doubt by this

time he has fully convinced the girl that she is the right-
ful heiress to property — as he stated to Scott —
valued at over a million dollars. That 's a stake worth
fighting for, and these two will make a hard combination. He 's got the papers, or claims to have, and they
must be the ones stolen from your father. I have been
trusting you might know something in your family history which would make it all plain."

"But I do not," decisively. "You must believe me;
not so much as a hint of any secret has ever reached me.
There are only the four of us, Father, Mother, Fred,
and I. I am sure there can be no secret; nothing which
I would not know. Perhaps, if I could see Miss
Maclaire —"

"I am convinced that would be useless," he interrupted, rising, and pacing across the floor. "If
Hawley has convinced her of the justice of the claim,
he will also have pledged her to secrecy. He is working out of sight like a mole, for he knows the fraud,
and will never come to the surface until everything
is in readiness. I know a better way; I 'll find Fred,
and bring him here. He would tell you whatever it was
he told Hawley, and that will give us the clue."

He picked up his hat from the table, but she rose
to her feet, holding forth her hands.

"I cannot thank you enough, Captain Keith," she

exclaimed frankly. " You are doing so much, and with no personal interest —"

" Oh, but I have."

The long lashes dropped over the brown eyes.

" What do you mean? "

" That I have a personal interest — in you, Hope."

She stood silent, her bosom rising and falling to rapid breathing.

" You don't mind my calling you Hope? I have n't got used to Miss Waite yet."

Her eyes met his swiftly.

" Of course, not. Such ceremony would be foolish after all you have done for me. Do — do you call her Christie? "

He laughed, clasping her hands closer.

" I assure you no — she is strictly Miss Maclaire, and," solemnly, " shall be to the end of the chapter."

" Oh, well, I did n't care, only that was what you called her when you were telling me what she said. Are you going? "

" Yes, to find Fred; the sooner we can get this straightened out, the better."

# CHAPTER XXIV

## A MISTAKE IN ASSASSINATION

LET his future be what it might, Jack Keith would never again forget the girl who held the door open for his passage with one hand, her other clasped in his. Interested before, yet forcing himself into indifference now that he knew who she really was, the man made full surrender. It was a struggle that kept him from clasping the slender figure in his arms, and pouring forth the words of tenderness which he sternly choked back. This was neither the time, nor the place, yet his eyes must have spoken, for Hope's glance fell, and her cheeks grew crimson.

" I do not need to pledge you to return this time, do I? " she questioned, her voice trembling.

" No," he answered, " nor any time again."

The hall was deserted, but a few men loitered in the office. Keith recognized none of the faces, and did not stop to make any inquiries of the clerk. It was growing dark, the lights already burning, and from the plashing of drops on the window, it must be raining outside. Hawley would surely have ended his call upon

Miss Maclaire long before this, and left the hotel. However interesting his communication might have proven, she must fill her evening engagement at the Trocadero, and would require time for supper and rest. As to the result of that interview there could be little doubt. Providing the gambler possessed the proper papers he would have small difficulty in convincing the girl that she was indeed the one sought. Keith had probed sufficiently into her mind to feel assured that her inclination was to side with Hawley. Under all the circumstances this was natural enough, and he did not blame her.

He glanced into the bar-room as he passed, not in any anticipation, but merely from the vigilance which becomes second nature upon the frontier. Hawley stood leaning against the bar, where he could see any-one passing through the hall. The eyes of the two men met, but the gambler never moved, never changed his attitude, although Keith noted that his right hand was hidden beneath the skirts of his long coat. The plainsman drew back, facing his enemy, until he reached the outer door. There was a sneer on Hawley's dark sinister face like an invitation, but a memory of the girl he had just left, and her dependence upon him, caused Keith to avoid an encounter. He would fight this affair out in a different way. As the door opened and he slipped forth into the gloom, he brushed against a man apparently just entering.  The gleam of light fell for an instant upon the face of the other — it was Scotty with the red moustache.

They had been watching for him then — what for? Hawley on the inside, and this man Scott without, were waiting to determine when he left the hotel; would probably dog his footsteps to discover where he went. Keith loosened his revolver, so as to be assured he could draw quickly, and slipped back into the shadow of the steps, his eyes on the door of the hotel.  There was a cold, drizzly rain falling, the streets almost deserted, appearing sodden and miserable where the lights shone forth through saloon windows.  One or two men, seeking supper, coat collars turned up and hats drawn low over their eyes, climbed the rickety steps and went in, but no one came out.  Perhaps he was mistaken as to the purpose of those fellows; they may have desired merely to know when he left, or Scott's return just at that moment might have been an accident.  To be sure, the hotel possessed a back exit, but he could not cover both ends of the building, and must take his chances.  It was too wet and disagreeable to remain crouched there, now that it was evident there was no intention of following him.  With hand on the butt of his gun, suspicious and watchful, yet with

15

scarcely a faster beat to his heart, Keith straightened up, and began splashing his way through the mud down the street. He knew where Willoughby would be most likely found at this hour — with cronies at the " Tenderfoot "— and he meant to discover the boy, and make him confess to Hope the truth. Matters had now reached a point where longer delay was dangerous.

Sheridan was seemingly dead, the long street silent, gloomy, black, except for those streams of saloon light shining across pools of water. He stumbled over the irregular ground, occasionally striking patches of wooden sidewalk or a strip of cinders. Here and there a tent flapped in the wind, which drove the drizzle into his face; somewhere ahead a swinging sign moaned as if in agony. A few wanderers ploughed through the muck, dim uncertain shapes appearing and vanishing in the gloom. He had gone a block and over, the struggle against the elements leaving him forgetful of all else, when a man reeled out of some dimly lit shack to his right, and staggered drunkenly forward a few feet in advance. He could barely distinguish the fellow's outlines, giving little thought to the occurrence, for the way was unusually black along there, the saloon opposite having shades drawn. Suddenly a flash of red fire spurted into the night, with a sharp report. It was so close at hand it blinded him, and he flung up one arm over his eyes, and yet, in that single instant, he perceived the whole picture as revealed by the red flame. He saw the man in front go down in a heap, the projection of the building from behind which the shot came, the end of a wagon sticking forth into the street which had concealed the assassin. The blinding flash, the shock of that sudden discharge, for a moment held him motionless; then he leaped forward, revolver in hand, sprang around the end of the wagon, and rushed down the dark alley between two buildings. He could see nothing, but someone was running recklessly ahead of him, and he fired in the direction of the sound, the leaping spurt of flame yielding a dim outline of the fugitive. Three times he pressed the trigger; then there was nothing to shoot at — the fellow had faded away into the black void of prairie. Keith stood there baffled, staring about into the gloom, the smoking revolver in his hand. The sound of men's voices behind was all that reached him, and feeling the uselessness of further pursuit, he retraced his way back through the narrow passage.

A group was gathered about the body in the rain, a single lantern glimmering. Two or three men had started down the passageway, and Keith met them, revolvers drawn and suspicious.

"Who are you?" snapped one sharply. "Were you doing all that shooting yonder?"

Keith recognized the voice, thankful that he did so.

"I fired at the fellow, but he got away onto the prairie. I reckon you could n't have done any better, Bill."

"Jack Keith!" and Hickock's voice had a new tone, his hand dropping on the other's shoulder. "Never was gladder to meet a fellow in my life. Boys, this is an old deputy of mine down in Dodge. When he gives up chasin' a murderer there is n't much use our tryin'. Let 's go back, and find out how bad the fellow is hurt. While we 're feelin' our way, Jack, you might tell us what you know about this affair."

"It was just the flash of a gun, and the man dropped," Keith explained, briefly. "I was ten or a dozen feet behind, and the fellow fired from under the wagon there. He must have been laying for some one — I reckon, maybe, it was me."

"You? Then it 's likely you have some notion who he was?"

"Well, if I have, Bill," and Keith's lips were set tight, "I 'm not liable to tell you. If it 's the lad I think likely, I 'll attend to the case myself. You understand — this is my personal affair."

Hickock nodded, his hand again pressing the other's shoulder.

" Sure, Jack, if you feel that way.   There 's enough doing here in Sheridan to keep a marshal reasonably busy, without dippin' into private matters.   I rather reckon you can take care of yourself, but if you need me, old boy, I 'm always right here on the job.   You know ,that."

" I do, Bill, and appreciate it."

The group about the motionless body fell away, and made room for the marshal, the last man to rise saying soberly:

" He 's dead all right, Hickock.   I guess he never knew what hit him.   Good shootin', too, dark as it is here."

" Had the range fixed, likely," returned the marshal. " That 's what makes it look like it was arranged for."

He bent down, striving to distinguish the dead man's features turned up to the drizzle, but the night revealed only the faintest outline.

" Anybody know him? "   There was no response, only a shuffling of feet in the mud.   " Here you man with the lantern, hold it over where I can see.   There, that is better.   Now, you fellows take a look, and see if some of you can't name the poor devil."

They glanced down, one after the other, over Bill's shoulder, shading their eyes from the rain so as to see clearer. The light of the flickering lantern streamed full on the ghastly face, but each man shook his head, and passed on. Keith hung back, hoping some one would identify the body, and not make it necessary for him to take part in the grewsome task. It was not likely to be any one he knew, and besides, he felt the man had died in his stead, and he dreaded to look upon the stricken face. When the last of the group had drifted back out of the radius of light, Hickock looked up, and saw him.

"Here, Jack," he said, gravely, " you better try — you might know him."

Keith bent over, and looked down. As he did so his heart seemed to rise choking into his throat, and a blur obscured his sight. He swept a hand over his eyes and dropped on his knees into the mud beside the body, staring speechless into the white face, the sightless eyes. Hickock watching him closely, and gripped his arm.

"What is it? Do you know him?"

"My God, yes; Fred Willoughby!"

# CHAPTER XXV

### A REAPPEARANCE OF THE GENERAL

KEITH did not inform Hope of her brother's death until the following morning, but had the body properly prepared for burial, and devoted the remainder of the night to searching for General Waite, and, incidentally, for both Hawley and Scott. Both Hickock and Fairbain assisted in this effort to learn the whereabouts of the dead boy's father, but without the slightest result, nor did Keith's investigations reveal the gambler at any of his accustomed resorts, while Scott had apparently made a complete get-away. These disappearances merely served to convince him as to the truth of his first suspicions; Scott might have departed for good, but Hawley would certainly reappear just so soon as assured his name had not been mentioned in connection with the tragedy. To Neb alone did the plainsman candidly confide his belief in the guilt of these two, and when other duties called him elsewhere, he left the negro scouring the town for any possible reappearance of either.

Heavy-eyed from lack of sleep, heavy-hearted with

his message, yet fully decided as to what advice he should offer, Keith returned to the hotel, and requested an interview with Hope. Although still comparatively early, some premonition of evil had awakened the girl, and in a very few moments she was prepared to receive her visitor. A questioning glance into his face was sufficient to assure her of unpleasant news, but, with one quick breath, she grasped his arm as though his very presence afforded her strength.

"How tired you look! Something has occurred to keep you out all night — and — and I know you have brought me bad news. Don't be afraid to tell me; I can bear anything better than suspense. Is it about father?"

"No, Hope," and he took her hand, and led her to a chair. Bending above her he gave her the whole story of the night, and she scarcely interrupted with a question, sitting there dry-eyed, with only an occasional sob shaking her slender form. As he ended, she looked up into his face, and now he could see a mist of unshed tears in her eyes.

"What shall I do, Captain Keith? I am all alone with this, except for you."

"I have considered that, Hope," he answered, gravely, "and it seems to me your present duty is more to the living than the dead. You should remain here until we learn something definite regarding your father, and discover the truth of this conspiracy formed against him. If Fred could know the trouble his chance words have caused, he would wish you to do this. With him gone, we are going to find the unravelling harder than ever. It is my judgment, Hope, your brother should be buried here."

She shuddered, her hands pressed to her eyes.

" Oh, on that horrible ' Boots Hill ' ? "

" Only temporarily, little girl," his voice full of deepest sympathy. " In a few weeks, perhaps, it could be removed East."

She was silent for what seemed to him a long while; then she looked up into his face, clinging to his arm.

" Yes," she said, " that will be best."

That same afternoon, the sun low in the west, they placed the dead boy in his shallow grave on " Boots Hill." It was a strange funeral, in a strange environment — all about the barren, deserted plains; far away to the east and west, the darker line marking the railroad grade, and just below, nestled close in against the foot of the hill, the squalid town of tents and shacks. There were not many to stand beside the open grave, for few in Sheridan knew the lad, and funerals were not uncommon — some cronies, half-drunk and maudlin, awed somewhat by the presence of the marshal, Doctor Fairbain, Keith, and Hope. That was all excepting the post chaplain from Fort Hays, who, inspired by a glimpse of the girl's unveiled face, spoke simple words of comfort. It was all over with quickly, and with the red sun still lingering on the horizon, the little party slowly wended their way back, down the steep trail into the one long street of Sheridan.

At the hotel Neb was waiting, the whites of his eyes shining with excitement, his pantomime indicating important news. As soon as he could leave Hope, Keith hurried down to interview his dusky satellite, who appeared about to burst with restrained information. As soon as uncorked that individual began to flow volubly:

" I sho' done seed 'em, Massa Jack; I done seed 'em both."

" Both?  Both who? "

" Massa Waite, sah, an' dat black debble dat we was huntin' fo'.  It was a mos' surprisin' circumstance, sah — a mos' surprisin' circumstance."

" Well, go on; where did you see them?  Do you mean they were together? "

The negro took a long breath, evidently overcome by the importance of his message, and unable to conjure up words wholly satisfactory to his ideas.

" It sho' am de strangest t'ing, Massa Jack, ebber
I prognosticated.  I was jest comin' roun' de corner
ob Sheeny Joe's shebang, back dar by de blacksmith
shop, when — de Lawd save me! — yere come ol'
Massa Waite, a ridin' 'long on a cream colo'd pinto just
as much alibe as ebber he was.  Yas, sah; he's whiskers
was blowin' round, an' I could eben yeah him cussin'
de hoss, when he done shy at a man what got up sudden like from a cart-wheel he was settin' on.  I done
took one look at dat secon' fellar, and seed it was dat
black debble from down Carson way.  Den I ducked
inter de blacksmith shop out 'er sight.  I sho' did n't
want Mister Hawley to git no chance at dis nigger —
I sho' did n't."

" Did they speak to one another? " Keith asked,
anxiously.  " Did you hear what was said? "

" Sho' dey talked, Massa Jack.  I sorter reckon dey
was dar for dat special purpose.  Sutt'nly, sah, dey
went right at talkin' like dey hed som't'ing on dey minds.
Ol' Massa Waite was a sittin' straight up on de hoss, an'
dat black debble was a standin' dar in front ob him.  Ol'
Massa Waite he was mad from de first jump off, an'
I could heah most eberyt'ing he said, but Mr. Hawley he grin de same way he do when he deal faro, an'
speaks kinder low.  De ol' man he swear fine at him, he
call him eberyt'ing — a damn liar, a damn scoundrel —

but Mr. Hawley he jest grin, and say ober de same ting."

" What was that, Neb? "

" Som't'ing 'bout a gal, Massa Jack — an' a law suit — an' how de ol' man better settle up widout no fightin'. I jest did n't git de whole ob it, he talked so low like."

" What did Waite say? "

" Well, mostly he jest cussed. He sho' told dat black debble 'bout what he thought ob him, but he did n't nebber once call him Hawley — no, sah, not once; he done call him Bartlett, or somet'ing or odder like dat. But he sutt'nly read dat man's pedigree from way back to de time ob de flood, I reck'n. An' he done swore he 'd fight for whatebber it was, papers or no papers. Den Hawley, he got plumb tired ob de ol' man swearin' at him, an' he grabbed a picter out ob he's pocket, an' says, ' Damn you; look at dat! What kind ob a fight can yo' make against dat face? ' De ol' man stared at it a while, sorter chokin' up; den he say softer like: ' It 's Hope; where did yo' ebber get dat? ' and de black debble he laughed, an' shoved de picter back into he's pocket. ' Hope, hell! ' he say, ' it 's Phyllis, an' I 'll put her before any jury yo 're mind to get — oh, I 've got yo' nailed, Waite, dis time.' "

" Was that all? "

" De ol' gin'ral he did n't seem ter know what ter

say; he done set dar lookin' off ober de prairie like he was clar flumegasted. He sho' did look like dat black debble hed hit him mighty hard. Den he says slow like, turnin' his hoss 'round: 'Bartlett, yo' am puttin' up a good bluff, but, by Gawd, I 'm goin' ter call yo'. Yo' don't get a cent ob dat money 'less yo' put up de proof. I 'll meet yo' whar yo' say, but ef I can git hol' ob some papers dat 's missin' I 'll take dat grin off yo' face.' De odder one laughed, an' de ol' gin'ral started fo' ter ride away, den he pull up he's hoss, an' look back. 'Yo' sorter herd wid dat kind ob cattle, Bartlett,' he say, sharp like, 'maybe yo' know a gam-bler roun' yere called Hawley?' De black debble nebber eben lose he's grin. 'Do yo' mean Black Bart Hawley?' 'Dat 's the man, where is he?' 'Dealin' faro fo' Mike Kenna in Topeka a week ago — friend ob yours?' 'Dat 's none ob yo' damned business,' snorted de ol' gin'ral, givin' his hoss de spur. Sho', Massa Jack, he nebber knowed he was talkin' ter dat same Hawley, an' dat black debble jest laughed as he rode off."

"When was all this, Neb?"

"'Bout de time yo' all went up on de hill, I reck'n. I done come right yere, and waited."

Keith walked across the room, selected a cigar, and came back, his mind busy with the problem. Hawley had in some manner, then, got into communication with Waite, and was threatening him. But Waite evidently knew the man under another name — his given name — and the gambler had sent him off on a false trail. The lost papers apparently contained the solution to all this mystery. Waite believed Hawley possessed them, but did not suspect that Bartlett and Hawley were the same person. What would he most naturally do now? Seek Hawley in Topeka probably; seize the first opportunity of getting there. Keith turned impatiently to the clerk.

" Any train running east? "

" Well, they generally start one out every day," with a glance toward the clock, " 'long 'bout this time. Maybe it 's gone, and maybe it has n't."

It was already nearly dark outside as the two men hastened toward the depot. They arrived there barely in time to see the red lights on the last car disappear. No inquiries made of those lounging about brought results — they had been interested in a lot of drunken graders loaded on the flat cars by force, and sent out under guard — and not one could tell whether any man answering Waite's description was in the single passenger coach. Convinced, however, that the General would waste no time in prosecuting his search, Keith believed him already on his way east, and after dismissing Neb, with instructions to watch out closely for Hawley, he made his own way back to the hotel.

It seemed strange enough how completely he was blocked each time, just as he thought the whole baffling mystery was about to be made clear. Hawley was playing in rare luck, all the cards running easily to his hand, thus, at least, gaining time, and strengthening his position. There could no longer be any doubt that the gambler possessed some knowledge which made him a formidable adversary. From Waite's statement it was the loss of the papers which left him helpless to openly resist the claim being made upon him on behalf of the mysterious Phyllis. His only hope, therefore, lay in recovering these; but, with time limited, he had been sent back on a wild goose chase, while Keith alone knew, with any degree of positiveness, where those documents really were. Hawley certainly had them in his possession the day before, for he had taken them to Miss Maclaire to thus convince her as to the truth of his statements. And Hawley was still in Sheridan. However, it was not likely the man would risk carrying documents of such value, and documents connecting him so closely with that murder on the Santa Fé Trail, about upon his person. At best, life was cheap in that community, and Black Bart must possess enemies in plenty. Yet if not on his person — where?

Scott was only a tool, a mere ignorant desperado, not to be trusted to such a degree — yet apparently he was the only one working with the gambler in this deal, the only one cognizant as to his plans. Christie — Keith came to a stop in the street at the recurrence of the woman's name. Why not? If she had been convinced, if she really believed that these papers proved her right to both property and parentage, then she would guard them as a tigress does her young. And Hawley would know that, and must realize they would be far safer in her hands than in his pocket. She could not use them without his aid and guidance, and yet, whatever happened to him, they would still be safely beyond reach. True, this might not have been done; the gambler might not yet have felt that he had sufficient hold upon the woman to trust her thus far, but it was, at least, a possibility to be considered, and acted upon.

Still wrestling with the intricate problem, Keith entered the dining-room, and weaved his way, as usual, through the miscellaneous crowd, toward the more exclusive tables at the rear. A woman sat alone at one of these, her back toward the door. His first thought was that it must be Hope, and he advanced toward her, his heart throbbing. She glanced up, a slight frown wrinkling her forehead, and he bowed, recognizing Christie Maclaire.

# CHAPTER XXVI

## A CHANCE CONVERSATION

THE opportunity thus so unexpectedly afforded was not one to be wasted, and Keith accepted it with swift determination. The expression in the woman's face was scarcely one of welcome, yet his purpose was sufficiently serious to cause him to ignore this with easy confidence in himself.

" I am, indeed, most fortunate to discover you alone, Miss Maclaire," he said, avoiding her eyes by a swift glance over the table, " and evidently at a time when you are only beginning your meal. May I join you? "

She hesitated for an instant, debating with herself, and as quickly deciding on disagreeable tactics.

" I presume this is a public table, and I consequently have little choice in the matter, if you insist," she replied, her voice more civil than her words. " Still, Mr. Keith, I am not accustomed to associating with criminals."

He smiled, holding his temper in check, more than ever determined to win.

" Then, possibly, you may rather welcome a new

diversion.   I can assure you our criminals out here are the most interesting portion of our population.   I wish I might have your permission."

Standing there before her, bare-headed, his slightly tanned face strong and manly, his gray eyes filled with humor, Miss Maclaire recognized again that he was not of the common herd, and the innate coquetry of her nature obtained mastery.   What harm could it do for her to chat with him for half an hour?   It was better than eating a lonely meal, and, besides, she might learn something of value to report to Hawley.   Her own eyes brightened, the slight frown disappearing.

"You are certainly an illustration of your theory," she said pleasantly.   "I shall have to say yes, but, really, I did not suppose you would enjoy being ranked among that class."

He drew out a chair, and sat down facing her, leaning slightly forward upon the intervening table.

"Nor would I, only I recognize you do not comprehend.   The source of your information is a bit polluted, Miss Maclaire.   There are those whose good opinion I do not seek, and you should not form your decisions on the unsupported testimony of a personal enemy."

"Oh, indeed," rather resenting the words, and already regretful of her compliance.   "Surely I have as much reason to trust my informant as I have you.   He, at least, has proven himself a friend."

" I wish I could feel as fully assured of that as you do," he returned honestly.   " I would then have every temptation to meddle further taken away from me. Do you realize that my interest is very largely upon your account? "

" Oh, no," laughing, " I could n't believe that.   I — I have heard it whispered it might be because of the other girl."

" The other girl! " in complete surprise at this swift return.

" Yes, sir," conscious of having attained the upper hand.   " Miss Hope Waite."

" Some more of Mr. Hawley's fancies," he retorted, perplexed that so much should be suspected.   " Have you seen her? "

" Why, of course.   I am a woman, Mr. Keith, with all the natural curiosity of my sex.   In this case I had special reason to be interested.   One does not meet her counterpart every day."

" The resemblance between you is certainly most striking."

" Sufficiently so," she said slowly, her eyes on his face, " to abundantly confirm in my mind the truth of all that has been told me."

The waiter approached with the orders, and the two remained in silence until he had deposited his load upon the table, and departed. She was watching the face opposite through lowered lashes that veiled her eyes, but Keith was first to break the stillness.

"I wish I might be told what that was."

"To what do you refer?" apparently forgetful as to where their conversation had been broken.

"To Hawley's proposition."

"No doubt," her lips smiling, "but you have come to the wrong market, Mr. Jack Keith."

"Yet," he insisted earnestly, "if this is all straight, with no fraud concealed anywhere, if you have the proofs in your hands, why are you afraid to talk openly. The very manner in which Hawley works should convince you he is himself afraid to face the truth."

"No, you are wrong. There are perfectly satisfactory reasons why we should for the present keep our plans secret. There are details yet to be decided upon, and Mr. Hawley's present objection to publicity is only ordinary prudence."

She leaned toward him, her fingers playing nervously with a knife.

"Mr. Keith, I cannot help but like you, and I also feel most kindly disposed toward Mr. Hawley. I wish in this I was no longer compelled to consider you an enemy to us both. There is no reason why I should, except for your blind prejudice against this other man who is my friend. I know you have some cause, for he has told me the entire story, yet I am sure he did no more than his actual duty. He let me realize how very sorry he was that the marshal at Carson City had called upon him for assistance."

"Who? Hawley?" Keith questioned, hardly trusting his own ears.

"Yes; indeed he is a very different man from what you have been led to believe. I know he is a gambler, and all that, but really it is not altogether his fault. He told me about his life, and it was very sad. He was driven from home when only a boy, and naturally drifted into evil company. His one ambition is to break away, and redeem himself. I am so anxious to help him, and wish you could realize his purpose, as I do, and become his friend. Won't you, for my sake? Why, even in this affair he has not the slightest mercenary purpose — he has only thought of what was rightfully mine."

Keith listened, feeling to the full the woman's earnestness, the impossibility of changing her fixed conviction. Hawley had planted his seed deep and well in fruitful soil.

"You make a strong and charming advocate, Miss

Maclaire," he returned, feeling the necessity of saying something. " I should like to have you equally earnest on my side. Yet it will be hard to convince me that ' Black Bart ' is the paragon of virtue you describe. I wish I might believe for your sake. Did he also explain how he came into possession of these papers? "

" Oh, yes, indeed; there is no secret about that. They were entrusted to him by an old man whom he discovered sick in Independence, and who died in his rooms three years ago. Mr. Hawley has been searching ever since for the old man's grand-daughter. It is remarkable how he was finally convinced that I was the one."

" A photograph, was it not? "

A gleam of sudden suspicion appeared in the brown eyes, a slight change in facial expression.

" That was a clue, yes, but far from being all. But why should I tell you this? — you believe nothing I say."

" I believe that you believe; that you are fully convinced of the justice of your claim. Perhaps it is just, but I am suspicious of anything which Bart Hawley has a hand in. Miss Christie, you really make me wish to retain your friendship, but I cannot do so if the cost includes faith in Hawley. Do you know that is not even his name — that he lives under an alias? "

" Is there anything strange in that out here? " she asked stoutly. " I told you how deeply he regretted his life; that alone would be sufficient cause for him to drop his family name. Did you ever learn his true name? "

He was not sure — only as Neb had reported what Waite had called the man, yet ventured a direct reply.

" Bartlett, I believe — he uses it now as a prefix."

" Bartlett! — Bartlett! " her hands clasping, and unclasping nervously. " Why, what a strange coincidence! "

" How? What do you mean? "

" Oh, nothing — nothing," biting her lips in vexation. " The name merely recalled something. But really I must go, Mr. Keith, or I shall be late at the theatre. You have not attended since I came? "

" No," arising from the table with her. " However, I have heard you sing before, and hope I may again."

" How tenderly you dwell on that word ' hope,' " she said banteringly, " it almost makes me envious."

" Your resemblance almost makes me forget."

" But not quite? "

" No, not quite," he confessed, smiling back into her quizzing eyes.

They went out into the hall together, only to meet

with Doctor Fairbain at the door. The latter stared at the two with some embarrassment, for a moment forgetful of his purpose. His gaze settled on the face of the lady.

"Always getting you two mixed," he blurted forth. "Never saw such resemblance — positively uncanny — same hotel too means trouble — this Miss Waite?"

"No, Doctor; I am Miss Maclaire."

"Ought to have known it — if I knew as much about faces as I do about anatomy never would make such mistake — very sorry — what fooled me was seeing you with Keith —thought he was after the other one — gay dog though — never satisfied — was hunting after you."

"After me?" evidently amused.

"Certainly — you — went to the room — then to the clerk — said you were in at supper — just occurred to me streets here bad at night — thought I 'd ask you to let me escort you to theatre and back — a bit of lunch later —" he glanced suspiciously at Keith — "probably got here too late."

"Well really you have, Doctor," she replied sweetly, veiling her eyes to hide their laughter. "But I can assure you it is not Mr. Keith," courtesying slightly to the latter, "for he has not honored me; we merely met by chance at the table. I am sure I should enjoy your company exceedingly, but to-night I must plead a previous engagement."

" Ah — ah, some other night? "

" With pleasure, yes."

The doctor faded away into the office, not wholly satisfied because Keith still lingered. Miss Christie extended her hand.

" Is n't he a funny man? But I do like him — someway I like so many people whom perhaps I ought not, including you, Mr. Jack Keith. Please think over what I told you about Mr. Hawley, won't you? "

" Certainly; you have given me food for thought. I presume he is to be your escort? "

She bowed, evidently resenting the question.

" Yes, and it may interest you to know that he has something of the utmost importance to tell me to-night — he has actually seen my guardian. Don't you wish you could be there? "

She gave him a tantalizing smile, withdrawing her hand, and running up the stairs before he could answer. Over the railing of the landing she glanced down, and then disappeared.

# CHAPTER XXVII

## MISS HOPE SUGGESTS

NO sooner had Miss Maclaire vanished than Keith's thoughts turned toward Hope Waite. She would need someone in her loneliness to take her mind from off her brother's death, and, besides, much had occurred of interest since the funeral, which he desired to talk over with her. Beyond even these considerations he was becoming aware of a pleasure in the girl's company altogether foreign to this mystery which they were endeavoring together to solve. He yearned to be with her, to look into her face, to mark how clearly the differing soul changed her from Christie Maclaire. He could not help but like the latter, yet somehow was conscious of totally different atmospheres surrounding the two. With one he could be flippant, careless, even deceitful, but the other aroused only the best that was in him, her own sincerity making him sincere.

Yet there was reluctance in his steps as he approached

the door of " 15," a laggardness he could not explain, but which vanished swiftly enough at Hope's greeting, and the sudden smile with which she recognized him.

" I was sure you would come," she declared frankly, " and I took an early lunch so as to be certain and be here.   It has seemed a long time since."

" And you might have even thought I had forgotten," he answered, releasing her hand reluctantly, " if you could have looked into the dining-room since, instead of staring out of these windows."

" Why?   How forgotten? " her eyes opening wide in surprise.

" I had the pleasure of taking supper with Miss Maclaire."

" Oh! " the exclamation decidedly expressive.

" Yes, I come at once to you with the confession. However, our meeting was purely accidental, and so I hope for pardon."

" Pardon from me?  Why, what difference can it possibly make to me? "

" Would you have me consort with the enemy? " he asked, scarcely daring to press his deeper meaning.

" Oh, no, of course not.   What did you talk about? Do you mind telling? "

" Not in the least; our conversation was entirely impersonal.   She was telling me about Hawley; what a

wonderfully good man he is. I have begun to suspect
the fellow has fascinated the poor girl — he is a good
looking devil, possessed of a tongue dripping with
honey."

"Surely you do not mean she has fallen in love with
him," and Hope shuddered at the thought. "Why
— why that would be impossible for — for a good
woman."

"Standards of morality are not always the same,"
he defended gravely. "Miss Maclaire's environment
has been vastly different from yours, Hope. She is
a variety hall singer; probably, from her own account,
a waif since childhood; and Hawley has come to her in
the character of a friend, appealing both to her interest and sympathy. I do not know she is in love with
him, I merely suspect she may be; certainly she is ready
to do battle on his behalf at the slightest opportunity.
She believes in him, defends him, and resents the slightest insinuation directed against him. He even escorts
her back and forth from her work."

"You know this?"

"I certainly do," and he laughed at the recollection.
"Fairbain met us coming out of the dining-room,—
you know what a delightful, blunt, blundering old fellow
he is! Well, Miss Christie must have made an impression even on his bachelor heart, for he actually re-

quested the privilege of escorting her to the Trocadero, and back to the hotel after the performance to-night — hinted at a lunch, the gay old dog, and pranced about like a stage-door Johnnie. It was a treat to watch her face when he blurted it all out, snapping his sentences as if he swung a whip-lash. She excused herself on the score of a previous engagement."

" But that was not necessarily with Hawley."

" I asked her directly, after the doctor had disappeared."

" You must have become very familiar," questioning once again in her voice.

" So Miss Maclaire evidently thought, judging from her manner. However she answered frankly enough, and, even defiantly, added the information that the gentleman had something to impart to her of the utmost importance, sarcastically asking me if I did n't wish I could be there and overhear. But sit down, Hope, until I tell you all that has occurred."

He went over the various events in detail, watching eagerly the expression upon her face as she listened intently, only occasionally interrupting with some pertinent inquiry. The light fell so that she sat partially in the shadow, where her eyes could not be read, yet he experienced no difficulty in comprehending the various moods with which she met his narrative, the color changing in her cheeks, her supple form bending toward him, or leaning backward in the chair, her fingers clasping or unclasping in nervous attention. He began with Neb's report, repeating, word by word, as nearly as he could recollect, what had passed between Hawley and her father. He paused to inquire if she had ever heard the name Bartlett, but her reply was merely a negative shake of the head. When he described their missing the train, she was, apparently, not convinced as to the General's departure upon it, although finally agreeing that, if he really believed the report that the man sought was elsewhere, it would be characteristic of him to accept the first means of getting there. "If he only knew I was here," she exclaimed wearily, "it might be so different, but, oh, we are all of us just groping in the dark." Then Keith turned to his chance meeting with Miss Maclaire, and repeated carefully their conversation, dwelling particularly upon the few admissions which had slipped through her lips. These did not seem important to either, although they treasured them up and talked them over. Then, having exhausted the topic, silence fell between them, Keith asking the privilege of lighting a cigar. Hope, after watching him apply the match, thinking what a fine face he had as the ruddy flame brought it forth with the clearness of a cameo, leaned back, drawing aside the semblance to a lace curtain, and staring forth, without seeing, into the street.

Somehow it was hard for her to fully realize the situation, and how closely it affected her. The swiftly passing events, the complication arising so suddenly, apparently out of nothing, left her feeling as though she must surely awake from a dream. She could not comprehend what it was all about; the names Bartlett and Phyllis had no clear meaning, they represented nothing but shadows; and this other woman — this music hall singer — what could there be in common between them? Yet there must be something — something of vital importance to her father — something which had already cost her brother's life. That was the one thing which made it seem an actuality — which brought it home to her as a rugged fact. But for that — and Keith — Keith sitting there before her — she would have doubted it all. And yet even Keith had come into her life so suddenly, so unexpectedly, as to leave her dazed and uncertain. So strongly did this feeling grip her in the silence, that she extended her hand and touched him, as though to make sure of his actual presence.

" What is it, Hope? "

" Oh, nothing — nothing," her voice breaking in a little sob. " It is so silly, but I was just wondering if you were real — everything seems so impossible. I cannot bring my mind to grasp the situation."

He did not smile, but only took the groping hand into both of his own.

" I think I understand, little girl," he said gravely. " You are totally unused to such life.   Almost without a moment's warning you have been plunged into a maelstrom of adventure, and are all confused. It is different with me — since the first shot at Sumter my life has been one of action, and adventure has grown to be the stimulus I need, and upon which I thrive. But I assure you," pressing the soft hand warmly, " I am real."

" Of course I know that; it makes me glad to know it.   If I could only do something myself, and not just sit here, it would all become real enough to me."

She rose suddenly to her feet, clasping her hands together, her face changing with new animation.

" Why could n't I?   I am sure I could.   Oh, Mr. Keith, it has just come to me how I can help."

He looked at her questioningly, thinking of her beauty rather than of what she said.

" Do — do I really appear so much like — like that woman? " she asked anxiously.

" Very much, indeed, excepting for the slight difference in age."

"That would never be noticed in the dark, or a poor light. Am I the same height?"

"Practically, yes."

"And my voice? — could you distinguish me from her by my voice?"

"I might; yet probably not, unless my suspicions were aroused. What is it you are thinking about?"

She took a deep breath, standing now directly facing him in the light.

"Of playing Miss Maclaire to-night," she said quickly. "Of taking her place, and learning what it is of so much importance Hawley has to report. Don't you think it might be done?"

The sheer audacity of this unexpected proposal left him speechless. He arose to his feet, gripping the back of the chair, almost doubting if he could have heard aright, his eyes searching the girl's face which was glowing with excitement. Of course he could not permit of her exposure to such a risk; the scheme was impracticable, absurd. But was it? Did it not offer a fair chance of success? And was not the possible result worthy the risk assumed? He choked back the earlier words of protest unuttered, puzzled as to what he had best say. A quick-witted resourceful woman might accomplish all she proposed.

"It looks so simple," she broke in impulsively, mov-

17

ing nearer him. "Don't you think I could do it? Would it be unwomanly?"

"The result, if accomplished, would abundantly justify the means, Hope," he acknowledged at last. "I was not hesitating on that account, but considering the risk you would incur."

"That would be so small — merely the short walk alone with him from the theatre to the hotel," she pleaded. "Once here it could make no difference if he did discover my identity, for there would be plenty of men near at hand to come to my defence. Oh, please say yes."

"If I do, then we must make the illusion perfect, and take as few chances of discovery as possible. I must learn exactly how the other dresses, and when she leaves the theatre. Fortunately for the success of your plan the Trocadero permits no one but performers to come behind the scenes, so that Hawley will be compelled to wait for the lady outside the stage door. I had better go at once, and see to these details."

"Yes," she said, her eyes sparkling with anticipation, "and I am so glad you are willing. I will be most discreet. You are not sorry I made the proposal?"

"Certainly not. At first it struck me as altogether wrong, but the more I think of it the stronger it appeals

to me. It may reveal to us the whole conspiracy, and
I cannot believe Hawley would venture upon any gross
familiarity likely to cost him the good opinion of his
ally. There is too much at stake. Wait here, Hope,
and I will be back the very moment I learn all that is
necessary."

A glance at the office clock convinced Keith that,
in all probability, Miss Maclaire had not, as yet, departed for the scene of her evening triumph. Still, it
could not be long before she would, and he lit a cigar,
sitting down in a corner partially concealed by the
clerk's desk to wait her appearance. This required
longer than anticipated, and fearing lest he might have
missed the departure entirely, he was about to question the busy Thomas, when he beheld Hawley enter
hurriedly from the street and run up the stairs. He
then had been the laggard. All the better, as he would
now have no opportunity to unfold his tale to the lady,
as it would be necessary for them to hurry to the theatre. Whatever the nature of the revelation it would
have to wait until the walk home. The excitement of
the adventure was already creeping into Keith's blood,
his pulse quickening.

The two returned almost immediately, conclusively
proving that Miss Maclaire, fully dressed for the
street, had been awaiting the arrival of her gallant with

some impatience.  Hawley was busily explaining his delay as they came down the stairs, and paid little attention to the seemingly deserted office.  Indeed, Miss Christie monopolized all his thoughts.  With quick scrutiny the watcher noted the more conspicuous articles of apparel constituting her costume — the white mantilla thrown over her head, the neatly fitting blue dress, the light cape covering the shoulders — surely it would not be difficult to duplicate these, so as to pass muster under the dim light of the streets.  Far enough in their rear to feel safe from observation he followed, noting with increased pleasure the rapidity with which they covered the required distance.  Clearly Miss Christie was already nervous lest she have not sufficient time remaining in which to properly dress for her act, and there would be no exchange of confidences on the outward journey.  Hawley left her, as Keith anticipated, at the stage entrance, the lady hastening within.  Her escort strolled leisurely back to the front of the house, and finally, purchasing a ticket, entered, the performance already having begun.

Keith knew perfectly the arrangement of the theatre — the seats in front; tables all through the centre; a gallery filled with benches; a noisy orchestra beneath the stage; a crowded audience of men, with only here and there a scattered representative of the gentler sex;

busy waiters dodging in and out among the tables, and down the aisles, filling orders for liquids from the nearby saloon. The air would be pungent with the odor of drink, thick with the fumes of tobacco, and noisy with voices, except as some special favorite on the stage won temporary attention. The Trocadero possessed but one redeeming feature — no doorway connected stage and auditorium, and the management brooked no interference with his artists. It had required some nerve to originally enforce this rule, together with a smart fight or two, but at this period it was acknowledged and respected. No sooner had Hawley vanished than Keith found occasion to enter into casual conversation with the door-keeper, asking a number of questions, and leaving impressed upon the mind of that astute individual the idea that he was dealing with a " gent " enamored of one of the stage beauties. A coin slipped quietly into the man's hand served to deepen this impression, and unlocked discreet lips otherwise sworn to secrecy. Out of much general information a little of real value was thus extracted — Miss Maclaire's act began at 9:45 and was over promptly at 10:10. It required about twenty minutes more for her to change again into street clothes, and she usually left the theatre immediately after, which would be about 10:30. Yes, there was a vestibule outside the stage door, and on bad nights, those waiting for the ladies could slip in there. But on such a night as this they generally hung around outside. No, there was no watchman, but the manager was frequently prowling around. He'd be busy, however, at 10:30, getting the stage ready for the "Flying Hermanns." Abundantly satisfied and resisting the door-keeper's professional suggestion that he'd better buy a ticket and take a look at the show, Keith slipped away, and hastened back to the hotel. The more he investigated the more feasible appeared the girl's plan, and he was now fully committed to it.

# CHAPTER XXVIII

## THE STAGE DOOR OF THE TROCADERO

HOPE discovered very little difficulty in duplicating the outer garments Keith reported Miss Maclaire as wearing. The colors, indeed, were not exactly the same, yet this difference was not sufficient to be noticeable at night by the eyes of a man who had no reason to suspect deceit. The girl was in a flutter of nervous excitement as she hastened about the room, donning her few requirements of masquerade, yet Keith noted with appreciation that she became perceptibly cooler as the moment of departure approached. With cheeks aflame and eyes sparkling, yet speaking with a voice revealing no falter, she pressed his arm and declared herself prepared for the ordeal. The face under the shadow of the mantilla was so arch and piquant, Keith could not disguise his admiration.

" Am I Christie Maclaire? " she asked laughingly.

" Sufficiently so to fool our friend," he returned, " but I am ready to swear that lady never looked so charming."

"A compliment, and spoken as though you really meant it."

"Have I not been honest enough with you in the past, to be credited with honesty now?" he protested, a little hurt by the bantering tone.

"Of course you have; I merely talk lightly to keep my courage up. You can have no idea how afraid I am."

"Then you are truly an actress, for you appear the picture of enjoyment. But we must go, or Hawley will be there before us, and thus spoil all our plans."

They passed out through the office together, seeing no one familiar to either, Hope keeping her face partially concealed. The east side of the street was less frequented than the other, having fewer saloons along its way, and they chose its darkness. As they advanced, the long habit of frontier life caused Keith to glance behind before they had progressed a block, and he was thus made aware that they were being followed. Conversing lightly, and without a word to alarm the girl, he yet managed to observe every movement of the dimly outlined figure which advanced with them, timing every motion to theirs. Long before they crossed the street to the Trocadero he was convinced there was no mistake — the fellow, whoever he might be, was trailing them. Keith smiled grimly to himself, resolving that, as soon as he had left the lady, he would teach the spy a lesson not soon to be forgotten.

They barely entered the outer circle of the Trocadero lights, noting a group of men thronging about the doors, and hearing the sound of the band within, and then turned swiftly down the narrow dark alleyway leading toward the stage entrance. Keith, having been there before, advanced confidently, but Hope, her heart beating wildly, clung to his arm, scarcely venturing a word in reply to his whispered assurances. Fortunately they encountered no one, and Keith, feeling cautiously in the dark, easily succeeded in locating the opening to the vestibule. Listening intently he became convinced that no one occupied the little shed. He had intended to remain with the girl until the time came for her to emerge, but the remembrance of that figure dogging them all the way from the hotel now caused a change of plan. He held her hand closely clasped in his.

"Now, Hope, I am going to leave you," he whispered, "and your own wit will have to carry you through. I know you will play your part all right, and it will be mine to wait for Christie, and give her some explanation of why Hawley failed to meet her as he promised. It will never do for her to suspect, until you have time to learn all possible. You are not afraid?"

" Yes, I am," clinging to him, " but — but I am going through it just the same."

" The truest kind of courage, my girl. Now slip
inside, but hold the door ajar. Hawley will certainly
be here within ten minutes, and you must join him at
once, or else the other might appear. You can judge
as to its being him even in this darkness. Good-bye."

The longing to clasp her in his arms, to speak the
language of his heart, was almost overwhelming, yet
the memory of that figure slinking along behind them,
and the brief time before Hawley's probable appearance,
for he would leave the theatre at the conclusion of Miss
Maclaire's act, restrained all demonstration. This
was a moment for action, not for words of love; no
delay should hazard the success of their undertaking.
He heard the slight creak of the door as the girl
slipped within the concealment of the vestibule, and
then he glided away through the darkness with the
stealthy silence of an Indian. There was no one in
the alley-way, which was narrow and easily explored,
but the glow from the front windows plainly revealed
the shadow of a man near the entrance, and Keith
slipped up toward him, hugging the side of the building for concealment, prepared to resort to harsh meas-
ures. As he reached out, gripping the astonished
loiterer by the collar, the two stared at one another in

surprise, and the gripping hand as instantly released its hold.

"You, Fairbain! What the devil does this mean? What are you spying on us for?"

Clearly taken aback, yet not greatly disturbed, his eyes showing pugnacious and his jaw set, the Doctor rubbed his throat where Keith's knuckles had left a red welt.

"Damn you, I think I'm the one to ask for an explanation," he growled. "She said she was not going with you, and now you are around here together at this hour. I had a right to know whether I was being played with like that."

"But, man, that was not Miss Maclaire I was with; it was Hope Waite. Come back here under the tent flap while I explain."

Fearful of the coming of Hawley he fairly dragged the portly figure of the bewildered Doctor with him, striving, by quickly spoken words, to make him comprehend the situation. Knowing previously something of the issues involved, it was not difficult to make Fairbain grasp the meaning of this present movement, yet his sympathies were at once enlisted upon the side of Miss Christie. He'd be damned if he would have any part in such a scheme — if she had a right to the money he'd help her get it — it was a cowardly trick, and he 'd fight if necessary, to keep her from becoming a victim. His voice rose, his arms brandishing violently, his sentences snapping like rifle shots. Keith angered, and fearful of a discovery which would leave Hope exposed, realized the futility of discussion and turned to physical force. Grasping the gesticulating man with both hands, he flung him backward and dragged him into the empty tent, kneeling on him as he throttled him to the earth.

"Now, Doctor, you listen to me," he said sternly. "I 'm through arguing. I hate to treat you like this, for you are my friend, but I 'll not stand for interference here. Do you get that, you old fool? Lie still until I get through! I respect your feelings toward Miss Maclaire. She is a good girl, and I hope to heaven you get her if you want her. But you never will if you permit this affair to go on. Yes, I know what I am talking about. In all that Hope and I do we are serving you and Christie,— our only fight is with 'Black Bart' Hawley. Stop being a bullet-headed old fool, Fairbain, and understand this thing. Lie still, I tell you, and hear me out! Hawley is a liar, a thief, and a swindler. There is a swindle in this thing somewhere, and he hopes to pull out a big sum of money from it. He is merely using Christie to pull his own chestnuts out of the fire. She is innocent; we realize that, but this fellow is going to ruin the girl unless we succeed in exposing him. He 's not only involving her in his criminal conspiracy, but he 's making love to her; he 's teaching her to love him. That 's part of his scheme, no doubt, for then she will be so much easier handled. I tell you, Fairbain, your only chance to ever win the interest of Christie Maclaire is to help us down this fellow Hawley. Yes, you can sit up; I reckon you 're beginning to see clearer, ain't you? "

Keith drew aside the flap of the tent to glance without, the light falling on Fairbain's face as he struggled to a sitting posture. He had had a new thought driven into him, yet failed to entirely grasp its significance.

" But, Jack," he asked, still half angry, " how about the girl? Has n't she any right to this money? "

" I don't know," honestly, " we don't any of us know, but whatever she has the right to she is going to get. You can bet on that, old man. We 're bucking Hawley not Christie Maclaire — get that into your head. He has n't any right, that 's certain, for he murdered and stole to get the papers — be quiet! Here the fellow comes now! "

They peered out together through the convenient tent flap, Fairbain scarcely less interested than the other, already dimly comprehending that his truly dangerous rival was the gambler, and that he could best serve the

lady by helping to prove to her the real character of
that individual.   He was still blindly groping in the
haze, yet out of Keith's sharp, stinging words there
had come to him a guiding light.   The latter gripped
his arm in restraint.

" Easy, old man, easy — let him pass."

Hawley turned into the alley whistling, evidently
well pleased with the situation and anticipating other
delights awaiting his coming.   The glow of the Trocadero's lights served, an instant, to reveal his face,
shaded by the broad brim of his hat, and then he vanished into the dark.   Keith leaning far out, yet keeping well within the shadows, heard the faint creak of the
vestibule door and the soft murmur of distant voices.
Then he drew back suddenly, his hand again grasping
Fairbain.   Two figures — those of a man and woman
— emerged into the dim light, and as quickly disappeared.   Apparently her hand was upon his arm, and
he was bending down so as to gain a glimpse of the face
partially concealed by the folds of the mantilla.   Only
a word or two reached them, a little laugh, and the
woman's voice:

" Why, of course I hurried; you said you had something of such importance to tell me."

" Fairbain," spoke Keith, his lips almost at the ear
of the other.   " That was Hope, all right, and she

has got him going already.   Now, man, will you help
us out?"

"I?   How?"

"Go back there, and meet Miss Maclaire.   I don't
care where you take her — lunch, anywhere; only keep
her from the hotel as long as possible.   You can do
it far better than I, for she will not suspect you of
any interest in this affair.   Tell her any lie you can
think up on account of Hawley's absence.   Good Lord,
old man, can't you see this is your chance; go in and
win."

Fairbain struggled to his feet, still a bit dazed and
uncertain, yet tempted by the opportunity.

"You're perfectly sure, Keith, this is n't anything
that will hurt the girl?"

"Sure!   Of course I am.   It's just Hawley I'm
gunning after.   For God's sake, have n't you got that
clear yet?"

"I — I reckon I'm an old fool, Jack," admitted
the Doctor regretfully, "and when an old fool is in
love he has n't got any sense left.   Anyhow I'll do what
you want me to now.   Where are you going?"

"To watch those others.   There is no knowing
what play Hawley might try to pull off, and I want to
keep within gun-shot of him.   Hurry up, man; that
vestibule door creaked just then."

He shoved him down the dark alley, and dodged back himself across the front of the tent out into the street. There was a crowd of men in front of the Trocadero, but the couple he sought were nowhere in sight.

# CHAPTER XXIX

## BY FORCE OF ARMS

WITH her heart throbbing fiercely, Hope clung to the outer door of the vestibule endeavoring to see a little of what was transpiring without. About her was dense darkness, and she dare not explore the surroundings. Behind could be heard, through what must have been a thin partition, the various distractions of the stage, shifting scenery, music, shuffling feet, voices, and the occasional sound of applause. The girl had nerved herself to the encounter with Hawley but this waiting here in darkness and uncertainty tried her to the uttermost. If some one should venture out that way how could she excuse her presence or explain her purpose? She found herself trembling in every limb from nervous fear, startled by every strange sound. Would the man never come? Surely Christie herself must be ready to depart by this time.

Almost prepared to flee before the terrors thus conjured up within her mind, they left her as if by magic the moment her straining eyes distinguished the approach of a dim figure without. She could not tell who it was, only that it was the unmistakable form of a man, and that he was whistling softly to himself. It might not prove to be the gambler, but she must accept the chance, for flesh and blood could stand the strain of waiting no longer. Yet she was not conscious of fear, only of exultation, as she stepped forth into the open, her blood again circulating freely in her veins. At the slight creak of the door the man saw her, his whistle ceasing, his hat lifted. Instantly she recognized him as Hawley, her heart leaping with the excitement of encounter.

"Why, hullo, Christie," he said familiarly, "I thought I was early, and expected a ten minutes' wait. I came out as soon as you left the stage."

"Oh, I can dress in a jiffy when there is any cause for hurry," Hope responded, permitting herself to drift under his guidance. "Are you disappointed? Would you prefer to commune with nature?"

"Well, I should say not," drawing her hand through his arm, and then patting it with his own. "I have seen about all I care to of nature, but not of Christie Maclaire."

"You may learn to feel the same regarding her," Hope answered, afraid to encourage the man, yet eagerly fearful lest she fail to play her part aright.

"Not the slightest danger," laughing lightly, and pressing her arm more closely against his body. "Although I must confess you exhibited some temper when I was late to-night."

"Did I not have occasion to? A woman should never be kept waiting, especially if her engagement be imperative."

"Oh, I am not finding any fault, you little spitfire. I like you all the better because you fight. But the trouble was, Christie, you simply jumped on me without even asking how it occurred. You took it for granted I was late on purpose to spite you."

"Well, were n't you?" and the girl glanced inquiringly up into his face, as they passed out of the alley into the light of the Trocadero's windows. "You certainly acted that way."

"No, I did not; but you would n't listen, and besides I had no time then to explain. There 's a lot happened this afternoon I want to tell you about. Will you give me time to talk with you?"

"Why, of course," surprised at the question, yet full of eagerness. "Why should you ask that?"

"Because I want you alone where no one can overhear a syllable. I 'm afraid of that damned hotel. You never know who is in the next room, and the slightest whisper travels from one end to the other.

That is one way in which Keith got onto our deal —
he had a room next to Willoughby and Scott, and overheard them talking.   I 'm not going to take any more
chances.   Will you go to ' Sheeny Joe's ' with me? "
    She drew back from him.
    " ' Sheeny Joe's ' ?   You mean the saloon near the
depot? "
    " Sure; what 's the use of being so squeamish?   You
sing and dance to a saloon crowd, don't you?   Oh, I
know you 're a good girl, Christie, and all that.   I 'm
not ranking you with these fly-by-nights around here.
But there 's no reason that I can see why you should
shy so at a saloon.   Besides, you won't see any one.
Joe has got some back rooms where we can be alone,
and have a bite to eat while we 're talking.   What do
you say? "
    " Oh, I would rather not," Hope faltered, bewildered
by this unexpected request, already half-tempted to
break away and run.   " Really I — I don't want to go
there."
    Hawley was evidently surprised at this refusal,
naturally supposing from her life that Miss Maclaire's
scruples would be easily overcome.   This obstinacy of
the girl aroused his anger.
    " You women beat the devil," he ejaculated, gruffly,
" pretending to be so damn particular.   Maybe you 'd

rather stand out there on the prairie and talk?" with a sweep of his hand around the horizon.

"Yes, I would," catching desperately at the straw. "I'm not afraid of you; I'm not blaming you at all, only I — I don't want to go to 'Sheeny Joe's.'"

He looked at her, puzzled at her attitude, and yet somewhat reassured by her expression of confidence. Oh, well, what was the difference? It might be better to let her have her own way, and the change would not materially interfere with his plans. Of course, it would be pleasanter sitting together at one of Joe's tables, but he could talk just as freely out yonder under the stars. Besides, it might be as well now to humor the girl.

"All right, Christie," his voice regaining its pleasant tone. "You shall have your way this time. There is too much at stake for us to quarrel over this."

Frightened, yet not daring to resist or exhibit the least reluctance, she clung to his arm, and permitted him to lead her to the right down a dark passage and out into the open land beyond. He had to feel his way carefully, and scarcely spoke, yet proceeded as though the passage was reasonably familiar and he had some definite point in view. She answered in monosyllables, now thoroughly regretful of having permitted herself to drift into this position, yet not in the least knowing how to extricate herself. Hawley took everything for

granted, her very silence convincing him of her acquiescence. With throbbing pulse, Hope felt the small
revolver hidden within her dress, undoing a button so
that, in emergency, she might grasp it more quickly.
Hawley felt the movement, the trembling of her arm.

"You are afraid, just the same," he said, pressing
her to him lover-like. "Darkness always gets on a
woman's nerves."

"Yes, that and loneliness," resenting his familiarity.
"Do we need to go any farther? Surely, we are
alone here."

"Only a few steps; the ravine is yonder, and we can
sit down on the rocks. I want to smoke, and we will
be entirely out of sight there."

He helped her down the rather sharp declivity until
both were thoroughly concealed below the prairie level.
Feeling about with his hands he found the surface of
a smooth rock, and seated her upon it. Then a match
flared, casting an instant's gleam across his face as he
lighted his cigar. Blacker than ever the night shut
down about them, and he groped for a seat beside her.
She could perceive just one star peering through a
rift of cloud, and in her nostrils was the pungent odor
of tobacco. With a little shiver of disgust she drew
slightly away from him, dreading what was to come.
One thing alone she felt was in her favor — however

familiar Hawley attempted to be, he was evidently not yet sufficiently sure of Miss Maclaire to become entirely offensive. She might not have frowned at his love-making, but apparently he had not yet progressed sufficiently far in her good graces to venture to extremes. Hope pressed her lips together, determined to resist any further approach of the man. However, his earliest words were a relief.

"I reckon, Christie," he said slowly, between puffs on his cigar, the lighted end of which faintly illumined his face, "you 've got the idea I have brought you out here to make love. Lord knows I 'd like to well enough, but just now there 's more important matters on hand. Fact is, my girl, we 're up against a little back-set, and have got to make a shift in our plans — a mighty quick shift, too," he added, almost savagely.

"I — I don't think I understand."

"No, of course, you don't. You imagine all we 've got to do in a matter of this kind is to step into the nearest court, and draw the money. One trouble is, our evidence is n't complete — we 've got to find that woman who brought you up."

"Oh!" said Hope, not knowing what else to say.

"Yes," he went on, apparently satisfied with her exclamation. "Of course, I know she 's dead, or at least, you say so, but we have n't got enough proof without her — not the way old Waite promises to fight your claim — and so we 've got to hunt for a substitute. Do you happen to know any old woman about the right age who would make affidavit for you? She probably would n't have to go on the stand at all. Waite will cave in as soon as he knows we 've got the evidence."

He waited for an answer, but she hardly knew what to say. Then she remembered that Keith insisted that Miss Maclaire had no conception that there was any fraud in her claim.

"No, I know no one. But what do you mean? I thought everything was straight? That there was no question about my right to inherit?"

"Well, there is n't, Christie," pulling fiercely on his cigar. "But the courts are particular; they have got to have the whole thing in black and white. I thought all along I could settle the entire matter with Waite outside, but the old fool won't listen to reason. I saw him twice to-day."

"Twice?" surprise wringing the word from her.

"Yes; thought I had got him off on a false scent and out of the way, the first time, but he turned up again like a bad penny. What 's worse, he 's evidently stumbled on to a bit of legal information which makes it safer for us to disappear until we can get the links of our chain forged. He 's taken the case into court already, and the sheriff is here tryin' to find me so as to serve the papers. I 've got to skip out, and so 've you."

" I? " rising to her feet, indignantly. " What have I done to be frightened over? "

He laughed, but not pleasantly.

" Oh, hell, Christie, can't you understand? Old Waite is after you the same way he is me. It 'll knock our whole case if he can get you into court before our evidence is ready. All you know is what I have told you — that 's straight enough — but we 've got to have proof. I can get it in a month, but he 's got hold of something which gives him a leverage. I don't know what it is — maybe it 's just a bluff — but the charge is conspiracy, and he 's got warrants out. There is nothing for us to do but skip."

" But my clothes; my engagement? " she urged, feeling the insistent earnestness of the man, and sparring for delay. " Why, I cannot go. Besides, if the sheriff is hunting us, the trains will be watched."

" Do you suppose I am fool enough to risk the trains? " he exclaimed, roughly, plainly losing patience. " Not much; horses and the open plains for us, and a good night the start of them. They will search for me first, and you 'll never be missed until you fail to show up at the Trocadero. Never mind the clothes; they can be sent after us."

" To-night! " she cried, awakening to the immediate danger, and rising to her feet. " You urge me to fly with you to-night? — now? "

" Sure, don't be foolish and kick up a row. The horses are here waiting just around the end of the ravine."

She pressed her hands to her breast, shrinking away from him.

" No! No! I will not go! " she declared, indignantly. " Keep back! Don't touch me! "

Hawley must have expected the resistance, for with a single movement he grasped her even as she turned to fly, pinning her arms helplessly to her side, holding her as in a vice.

" Oh, but you will, my beauty," he growled. " I thought you might act up and I 'm ready. Do you think I am fool enough to leave you here alone to be pumped dry? It is a big stake I 'm playing after, girl, and I am not going to lose it through the whims of a woman. If you won't go pleasantly, then you 'll go by force. Keep still, you tigress! Do you want me to choke you? "

She struggled to break loose, twisting and turning, but the effort was useless. Suddenly he whistled sharply. There was the sound of feet scrambling down the path, and the frightened woman perceived the dim outlines of several approaching men. She gave one scream, and Hawley released his grip on her arms to grasp her throat.

She jerked away, half-stumbling backward over a rock. The revolver, carried concealed in her dress, was in her hand. Mad with terror, scarcely knowing what she did, she pulled the trigger. In the flash she saw one man throw up his hands and go down. The next instant the others were upon her.

## CHAPTER XXX

### IN CHRISTIE'S ROOM

KEITH swept his glance up and down the street without results. Surely, Hawley and his companion could not have disappeared so suddenly. They had turned to the right, he was certain as to that, and he pushed through the crowd of men around the theatre entrance, and hastened to overtake them. He found nothing to overtake — nowhere along that stretch of street, illumined by window lights, was there any sign of a man and woman walking together. He stopped bewildered, staring blindly about, failing utterly to comprehend this mysterious vanishing. What could it mean? What had happened? How could they have disappeared so completely during that single moment he had waited to speak to Fairbain? The man's heart beat like a trip-hammer with apprehension, a sudden fear for Hope taking possession of him. Surely the girl would never consent to enter any of those dens along the way, and Hawley would not dare resort to force in the open street. The very thought seemed preposterous, and yet, with no other

284

supposition possible, he entered these one after the other in hasty search, questioning the inmates sharply, only to find himself totally baffled — Hawley and Hope had vanished as though swallowed by the earth. He explored dark passage-ways between the scattered buildings, rummaging about recklessly, but came back to the street again without reward.

Could they have gone down the other side, in the deeper shadows, and thus reached the hotel more quickly than it seemed to him possible? There was hardly a chance that this could be true, and yet Keith grasped at it desperately, cursing himself for having wasted time. Five minutes later, breathless, almost speechless with anxiety, he startled the clerk.

" Has Miss Waite come in? Miss Hope Waite? "

" Blamed if I know," retorted the other, indifferently. " Can't for the life of me tell those two females apart. One of them passed through 'bout ten minutes ago; Doc Fairbain was with her. Another party just went upstairs hunting Miss Maclaire, and as they have n't come down, I reckon it must have been her — anything wrong? "

" I 'm not sure yet," shortly. " Who was this other person? "

" Old fellow with white hair and whiskers — swore like a pirate — had the sheriff along with him."

It came to Keith in a flash — it was Waite. Perhaps Christie knew. Perhaps the General knew. Certainly something of importance was crystallizing in the actress' room which might help to explain all else. He rushed up the stairs, barely waiting to rap once at the closed door before he pressed it open. The sight within held him silent, waiting opportunity to blurt out his news. Here, also, was tragedy, intense, compelling, which for the instant seemed to even overshadow the fate of the girl he loved. There were three men present, and the woman. She stood clutching the back of a chair, white-faced and open-eyed, with Fairbain slightly behind her, one hand grasping her arm, the other clinched, his jaw set pugnaciously. Facing these two was Waite, and a heavily built man wearing a brown beard, closely trimmed.

"You 'd better acknowledge it," Waite snapped out, with a quick glance at the newcomer. "It will make it all the easier for you. I tell you this is the sheriff, and we 've got you both dead to rights."

"But," she urged, "why should I be arrested? I have done nothing."

"You 're an adventuress — a damn adventuress — Hawley's mistress, probably — a —"

"Now, see here, Waite," and Fairbain swung himself forward, "you drop that. Miss Maclaire is my friend, and if you say another word I 'll smash you, sheriff or no sheriff."

Waite glared at him.

" You old fool," he snorted, " what have you got to do with this ? "

" I 've got this to do with it, you 'll find — the woman is to be treated with respect or I 'll blow your damned obstinate head off."

The sheriff laid his hand on Waite's shoulder.

" Come," he said, firmly, " this is no way to get at it. We want to know certain facts, and then we can proceed lawfully. Let me question the woman."

The two older men still faced one another belligerently, but Keith saw Christie draw the doctor back from between her and the sheriff.

" You may ask me anything you please," she announced, quietly. " I am sure these gentlemen will not fight here in my room."

" Very well, Miss Maclaire. It will require only a moment. How long have you known this man Hawley ? "

" Merely a few days — since I arrived in Sheridan."

" But you were in communication with him before that ? "

The pleasant voice and quiet demeanor of the **sheriff** seemed to yield the girl confidence and courage.

" Yes, he had written me two or three letters."

" You met him here then by appointment? "

" He was to come to Sheridan, and explain to me more fully what his letters had only hinted at."

" You possessed no previous knowledge of his purpose? "

" Only the barest outline — details were given me later."

" Will you tell us briefly exactly what Hawley told you? "

The girl's bewildered eyes wandered from face to face, then returned to the waiting sheriff.

" May — may I sit down? " she asked.

" Most certainly; and don't be afraid, for really we wish to be your friends."

She sank down into the chair, and even Keith could see how her slender form trembled. There was a moment's silence.

" Believe me, gentlemen," she began, falteringly, " if there is any fraud, any conspiracy, I have borne no conscious part in it. Mr. Hawley came to me saying a dying man had left with him certain papers, naming one, Phyllis Gale, as heiress to a very large estate in North Carolina, left by her grandfather in trust. He said the girl had been taken West, when scarcely two

years old, by her father in a fit of drunken rage, and
then deserted by him in St. Louis."

"You — you saw the papers?"    Waite broke in.

"Yes, those that Hawley had; he gave them to me
to keep for him."    She crossed to her trunk, and came
back, a manilla envelope in her hand.    Waite opened
it hastily, running his eyes over the contents.

"The infernal scoundrel!" he exclaimed, hotly.
"These were stolen from me at Carson City."

"Let me see them."    The sheriff ran them over,
merely glancing at the endorsements.

"Just as you represented, Waite," he said, slowly.
"A copy of the will, your commission as guardian, and
memoranda of identification.    Well, Miss Maclaire,
how did you happen to be so easily convinced that you
were the lost girl?"

"Mr. Hawley brought me a picture which he said
was of this girl's half-sister; the resemblance was most
startling.    This, with the fact that I have never known
either father or mother or my real name, and that my
earlier life was passed in St. Louis, sufficed to make
me believe he must be right."

"You — you —" Waite choked, leaning forward.
"You don't know your real name?"

"No, I do not," her lips barely forming the

19

words.  " The woman who brought me up never told me."

" Who — who was the woman ? "

" A Mrs. Raymond — Sue Raymond — she was on the stage, and died in Texas — San Antonio, I think."

Waite swore audibly, his eyes never once deserting the girl's face.

" Hawley told you to say that ? "

" No, he did not," she protested warmly.  " It was never even mentioned between us — at least, not Sue Raymond's name.  What difference can that make ? "

He stepped forward, one hand flung out, and Fairbain sprang instantly between them, mistaking the action.

" Hands off there, Waite," he commanded, sternly. " Whatever she says goes."

" You blundering old idiot," the other exploded. " I 'm not going to hurt her; stand aside, will you ! "

He reached the startled girl, thrust aside the dark hair combed low over the neck, swung her about toward the light, and stared at a birthmark behind her ear. No one spoke, old Waite seemingly stricken dumb, the woman shrinking away from him as though she feared he was crazed.

" What is it ? " asked the sheriff, sternly.

Slowly Waite turned about and faced him, running

the sleeve of his coat across his eyes.  He appeared dazed, confounded.

"My God, it 's all right," he said, with a choke in the throat.  "She 's — she 's the girl."

Christie stared at him, her lips parted, unable to grasp what it all meant.

"You mean I — I am actually Phyllis Gale?  That — that there is no mistake? "

He nodded, not yet able to put it more clearly into words.  She swayed as though about to faint, and Fairbain caught her, but she slipped through his arms, and fell upon her knees, her face buried in her hands upon the chair.

"Oh, thank God," she sobbed, "thank God!  I know who I am!  I know who I am! "

# CHAPTER XXXI

## THE SEARCH FOR THE MISSING

THE note of unrestrained joy of relief in the woman's voice rang through the room, stilling all else, and causing those who heard to forget for an instant the sterner purpose of their gathering. Fairbain bent over her, like a fat guardian angel, patting her shoulder, her eyes so blurred with tears as to be practically sightless, yet still turned questioningly upon Waite. The sheriff was first to recover speech, and a sense of duty.

"Then this lets Miss Maclaire out of the conspiracy charge," he said, gravely, "but it does n't make it any brighter for Hawley so far as I can see — there 's a robbery charge against him if nothing else. Any one here know where the fellow is?"

For a moment no one answered, although Keith took a step forward, reminded instantly of Hope's predicament. Before he could speak, however, Christie looked up, with swift gesture pushing back her loosened hair.

"He was to have met me at the theatre to-night,"

she said, her voice trembling, " but was not there when I came out; he — he said he had important news for me."

" And failed to show up — did he send no message? "

" Doctor Fairbain was waiting for me instead. He said that Mr. Hawley was called suddenly out of town."

The eyes of the sheriff turned to Fairbain, whose face grew redder than usual, as he shifted his gaze toward Keith.

" That was a lie," he confessed, lamely. " I — I was told to say that."

" Just a moment, Sheriff," and Keith stood before them, his voice clear and convincing. " My name is Keith, and I have unavoidably been mixed up in this affair from the beginning. Just now I can relieve the doctor of his embarrassment. Miss Hope Waite and I have been associated together in an effort to solve this mystery. This evening, taking advantage of the remarkable resemblance existing between herself and Miss Maclaire, Miss Hope decided upon a mask —"

" What's that," Waite broke in excitedly. " Is Hope here? "

" Yes, has been for a week; we 've had all the police force of Sheridan hunting you."

The old man stared at the speaker, open-mouthed, and muttered something about Fort Hays, but Keith, paying little attention to him, hurried on with his story.

"As I say, she decided upon impersonating Christie here, hoping in this way to learn more regarding Hawley's plans. We had discovered that the two were to meet after the evening performance at the stage door of the Trocadero. I escorted Hope there, dressed as near like Miss Maclaire as possible, and left her inside the vestibule waiting for 'Black Bart' to appear. At the head of the alley I ran into Fairbain, told him something of the circumstances, and persuaded him to escort Miss Christie back to the hotel. He was not very hard to persuade. Well, Hawley came, and Hope met him; they went out of the alleyway together arm in arm, talking pleasantly, and turned this way toward the hotel. The doctor and I both saw and heard them. I was delayed not to exceed two minutes, speaking a final word to Fairbain, and when I reached the street they had disappeared. I have hunted them everywhere without finding a trace — I have even been through the resorts. She has not returned to the hotel, and I burst in upon you here hoping that Miss Maclaire might have some information."

She shook her head, and Waite, glaring impotently at the two of them, swore sharply.

" Good God, man! my girl! Hope, alone with that damn villain. Come on, Sheriff; we 've got to find her. Wait though! " and he strode almost menacingly across the room. " First, I want to know who the devil you are? "

Keith straightened up, looking directly into the fierce questioning eyes.

" I have told you my name — Jack Keith," he replied, quietly. " Doctor Fairbain knows something of me, but for your further information I will add that when we met before I was Captain Keith, Third Virginia Cavalry, and bearing despatches from Longstreet to Stonewall Jackson."

The gruff old soldier, half-crazed by the news of his daughter's peril, the gleam of his eyes still revealing uncontrolled temper, stared at the younger face fronting him; then slowly he held out his hand.

" Keith — Keith," he repeated, as though bringing back the name with an effort. " By God, that 's so — old Jefferson Keith's boy — killed at Antietam. And you know Hope? "

" Yes, General."

He looked about as though dazed, and the sheriff broke in not unkindly.

" Well, Waite, if we are going to search for your

daughter we better be at it. Come on, all of you; Miss Maclaire will be safe enough here alone."

He took hold of Keith's arm, questioning him briefly as they passed down the hall. On the stairs the latter took his turn, still confused by what he had just heard.

"Who is Miss Maclaire?" he asked.

"Phyllis Gale."

"Of course, but who is Phyllis Gale? What has she to do with General Waite? His daughter has told me she never heard of any one by that name."

"Well, Keith, the old man has never told me very much; he's pretty close-mouthed, except for swearing, but I've read his papers, and picked up a point or two. I reckon the daughter, Miss Hope, maybe never heard a word about it, but the boy — the one that was shot — must have stumbled onto the story and repeated it to Hawley. That's what set that fellow going. It seems Mrs. Waite's maiden name was Pierpont, and when she was seventeen years old she was married to the son of a rich North Carolina planter. The fellow was a drunken, dissolute good-for-nothing. They had a daughter born — this Phyllis — and when the child was three years old her father, in a fit of drunken rage, ran away, and to spite his wife took the little girl with him. All efforts to trace them failed, and the mother finally secured a divorce and, two years later, married Willis Waite. Waite, of course, knew these facts, but probably they were never told to the children. When the father of Mrs. Waite's first husband died, he left all his large property to his grandchild, providing she could be found and identified within a certain time, failing which the property was to be distributed among certain designated charities. Waite was named sole administrator. Well, the old man took as much interest in it as though it was his own girl, but made mighty little progress. He did discover that the father had taken the child to St. Louis and left her there with a woman named Raymond, but after the woman died the girl completely disappeared."

"Then Miss Maclaire is Hope Waite's half-sister?"

"That's the way it looks now."

"And Hawley merely happened to stumble on to the right party?"

"Sure; it's clear enough how that came about. The boy told him about the lost heiress his father was searching after, and showed him his sister's picture. 'Black Bart' instantly recognized her resemblance to Christie Maclaire, and thought he saw a good chance for some easy money. He needed the papers, however, to ascertain exactly the terms of the will, and what would be necessary for the identification. He never intended to go into court, but hoped to either get Waite out of the way, or else convince him that Christie was the girl, relying on her gratitude for his profits. When Waite played into his hands by coming to Carson City, the chance was too good to be lost. I 'm not sure he meant to kill him, but he did mean to have those papers at any cost. Probably you know the rest — the girl was easy, because she was so ignorant of her parentage, and nothing prevented Hawley from winning except that Waite got mad and decided to fight. That knocked over the whole thing."

They were outside now, and the first touch of the cool night air, the first glance up and down the noisy street, brought Keith to himself, his mind ready to grapple with the problem of Hope's disappearance. It seemed to him he had already looked everywhere, yet there was nothing to do except to continue the search, only more systematically. The sheriff assumed control — clear headed, and accustomed to that sort of thing — calling in Hickock and his deputies to assist, and fairly combing the town from one end to the other. Not a rat could have slipped unobserved through the net he dragged down that long street, or its intersecting alleys — but it was without result; nowhere was there found a trace of either the gambler or his companion.

They dug into saloons, bagnios, dance-halls, searching back rooms and questioning inmates; they routed out every occupant of the hotel, invaded boarding houses, and explored shacks and tents, indifferent to the protests of those disturbed, — but without result. They found several who knew Hawley, others who had seen the two together passing by the lighted windows of the Trocadero, but beyond that — nothing. Convinced, at last, that the parties sought were not alive in Sheridan, and beginning to fear the worst, the searchers separated, and began spreading forth over the black surrounding prairie, and by the light of lanterns seeking any semblance of trail. There was no lack of volunteers for this work, but it was daylight before the slightest clue presented itself. Keith, with the sheriff and two or three others, had groped their way outward until, with the first flush of dawn, they found themselves at the opening of a small rocky ravine, near the foot of " Boots Hill." Peering down into its still shadowed depths, they discerned what appeared like a body lying there motionless. Keith sprang down beside it, and turned the rigid form over until the dead face was revealed in the wan light —

it was that of the red moustached Scott.   He staggered back at the recognition, barely able to ejaculate.

"Here, Sheriff!   This is one of Hawley's men!"

The sheriff was bending instantly above the corpse, searching for the truth.

"You know the fellow?"

"Yes, his name was Scott."

"Well, he's been dead some hours, at least six I should say; shot just above the eye, and good Heavens! look here, Keith, at the size of this bullet wound; that's no man's gun in this country — no more than a '32' I'd say."

"Miss Waite had a small revolver.  She must have shot the fellow.  But why did they leave the body here to be discovered?"

The sheriff arose to his feet, prowling about in the brightening glow of the dawn.

"They were in a hurry to get away, and knew he wouldn't be found before morning.  A six hours' start means a good deal.  They did drag him back out of sight — look here.  This was where the struggle took place, and here is where the man fell," tracing it out upon the ground.  "The girl put up a stiff fight, too — see where they dragged her up the path.  From the footprints there must have been half a dozen in the party. Get back out of the way, Sims, while I follow their trail."

It was plain enough, now they had daylight to assist them, and led around the edge of the hill. A hundred feet away they came to where horses had been standing, the trampled sod evidencing they must have been there for some considerable time. Keith and the sheriff circled out until they finally struck the trail of the party, which led forth southwest across the prairie.

" Seven horses, one being led light," said the former. " That was Scott's, probably."

" That 's the whole story," replied the sheriff, staring off toward the bare horizon, " and the cusses have at least six hours the start with fresh horses." He turned around. " Well, boys, that takes 'em out of my baliwick, I reckon. Some of the rest of you will have to run that gang down."

# CHAPTER XXXII

### FAIRBAIN AND CHRISTIE

D R. FAIRBAIN had originally joined the searching party, fully as eager as Keith himself to run down the renegade Hawley, but after an hour of resultless effort, his entire thought shifted to the woman they had left alone at the hotel. He could not, as yet, fully grasp the situation, but he remained loyal to the one overpowering truth that he loved Christie Maclaire. Fairbain's nature was rough, original, yet loyal to the core. He had lived all his life long in army camps, and upon the frontier, and his code of honor was extremely simple. It never once occurred to him that Christie's profession was not of the highest, or that her life and associations in any way unfitted her for the future. To his mind she was the one and only woman. His last memory of her, as the little party of men filed out of that room, haunted him until he finally dropped out of the search, and drifted back toward the hotel.

It was a late hour, yet it was hardly likely the woman had retired. Her excitement, her interest in the pursuit, would surely prevent that; moreover, he was certain he saw a light still burning in her room, as he looked up from the black street below. Nevertheless he hesitated, uncertain of his reception. Bluff, emphatic, never afraid to face a man in his life, his heart now beat fiercely as he endeavored to muster the necessary courage. Far down the dark street some roysterer fired a shot, and sudden fear lest he might be sought after professionally sent the doctor hurriedly within, and up the stairs. He stood, just outside her door, quaking like a child, the perspiration beading his forehead, but a light streamed through the transom, and he could plainly hear movements within. At last, in a sudden spasm of courage, he knocked softly. Even in that noisy spot she heard instantly, opening the door without hesitation, and standing fully dressed within. She was no longer a discouraged, sobbing girl, but an aroused, intent woman, into whose pathetic, lonely life there had come a new hope. She appeared younger, fairer, with the light shimmering in her hair and her eyes smiling welcome.

"Oh, Doctor," and her hands were thrust out towards him, "I am glad you have come. Somehow, I thought you would, and I have wanted so to talk to someone — to you."

"To me! Do you really mean that, Miss Christie?"

" Yes, I really mean that, you great bear of a man," and the girl laughed lightly, dragging him into the room, and closing the door. " Why, who else could I expect to come to-night? You were the only one really good to me. You — you acted as if you believed in me all the time —"

" I did, Christie; you bet I did," broke in the delighted doctor, every nerve tingling. " I 'd 'a' cleaned out that whole gang if you 'd only said so, but I reckon now it was better to let them tell all they knew. It was like a thunder storm clearing the atmosphere."

" Oh, it was, indeed! Now I know who I am — who I am! Is n't that simply glorious? Sit down, Doctor Fairbain, there in the big chair where I can see your face. I want to talk, talk, talk; I want to ask questions, a thousand questions; but it would n't do any good to ask them of you, would it? You don't know anything about my family, do you? "

" Not very much, I am afraid, only that you have got an almighty pretty half-sister," admitted the man, emphatically, " and old Waite possesses the vilest temper ever given a human being. He 's no blood kin to you, though."

" No, but he is awfully good underneath, isn't he? "

" Got a heart of pure gold, old Waite. Why, I 've

seen him cry like a baby over one of his men that got hurt."

" Have you known him, then, for a long while? "

" Ever since the Spring of '61. I was brigaded with him all through the war, and had to cut a bullet or so out of his hide before it ended. If there was ever a fight, Willis Waite was sure to get his share. He could swear some then, but he 's improved since, and I reckon now he could likely claim the championship."

" Did — did you know my mother also? " and Christie leaned forward, her eyes suddenly grown misty. " I have n't even the slightest memory of her."

The doctor's heart was tender, and he was swift to respond, reaching forth and grasping the hand nearest him. He had made love before, yet somehow this was different; he felt half afraid of this woman, and it was a new sensation altogether, and not unpleasant.

" I saw her often enough in those days, but not since. She was frequently in camp, a very sweet-faced woman; you have her eyes and hair, as I remember. Waite ought to have recognized you at first sight. By Heavens! that was what made me so infernally mad, the mulish obstinacy of the old fool. Your mother used to come to the hospital tent, too; one of the best nurses I ever saw. I thought she was a beauty then,

20

but she's some older by this time," he paused regretfully. "You see, I'm no spring chicken, myself."

Her eyes were upon his face, a slight flush showing in either cheek, and she made no effort to withdraw her imprisoned hand.

"You are just a nice age," with firm conviction. "Boys are tiresome, and I think a little gray in the hair is an improvement. Oh, you mustn't imagine I say this just to please you — I have always thought so, since — well, since I grew up. Besides, fleshy men generally look young, because they are so good natured, perhaps. How old are you, Doctor?"

"It isn't the gray hairs I mind, either," he admitted hesitatingly, "but I'm too darned bald-headed. Oh, I ain't so old, for I was only thirty-five when the war broke out. I was so thin then I could hardly cast a shadow. I've changed some since," casting his eyes admiringly downward, "and got quite a figure. I was forty-three last month."

"That isn't old; that's just right."

"I've been afraid you looked on me as being an old fogy!"

"I should say not," indignantly. "Why should you ever think that?"

"Well, there were so many young fellows hanging about."

" Who ? "

" Oh, Keith, and Hawley, and that bunch of officers from the fort; you never had any time to give me."

She laughed again, her fingers tightening in their clasp on his hand.

" Why, how foolish; Hawley is older than you are, and I was only playing with Keith.  Surely you must know that now.  And as to the officers, they were just fun.  You see, in my profession, one has to be awfully nice to everybody."

" But did n't you really care for Hawley? " he insisted, bluntly probing for facts.

" He — he interested me," admitted the girl, hesitatingly, her eyes darkening with sudden anger.  " He lied and I believed him — I would have believed any one who came with such a story.  Oh, Dr. Fairbain," and she clung to him now eagerly, " you cannot realize how hungry I have been for what he brought me.  I wanted so to know the truth of my birth.  Oh, I hated this life ! "  She flung her disengaged hand into the air, with a gesture expressive of disgust.  " I was crazy to get away from it.  That was what made the man look good to me — he — he promised so much.  You will believe me, won't you?  Oh, you must; I am going to make you.  I am a singer in music halls; I was brought up to that life from a little girl, and of course,

I know what you Western men think of us as a class. Hawley showed it in his whole manner toward me, and I resented it; just for that, deep down in my heart, I hated him. I know it now, now that I really understand his purpose; but some way, when I was with him he seemed to fascinate me, to make me do just as he willed. But you have never been that way; you — you have acted as though I was somebody — somebody nice, and not just a music-hall singer. Perhaps it 's just your way, and maybe, deep down you don't think I 'm any better than the others do, but — but I want you to think I am, and I am going to tell you the truth, and you must believe me — I am a good girl."

"Great God! of course you are," he blurted out. "Don't you suppose I know? That is n't what has been bothering me, lassie. Why, I 'd 'a' fought any buck who 'd 'a' sneered at you. What I wanted to know was, whether or not you really cared for any of those duffers. Can you tell me that, Christie?"

She lifted her eyes to his face, her lips parted.

"I can answer any thing you ask."

"And you do not care for them?"

"No."

He drew his breath sharply, his round face rosy.

"Then you have got to listen to me, for I 'm deadly in earnest. I 'm an old, rough, bald-headed fool that don't know much about women,— I never thought before I 'd ever want to,— but you can bet on one thing, I 'm square.   Anybody in this town will tell you I 'm square.   They 'll tell you that whatever I say goes. I 've never run around much with women; somehow I never exactly liked the kind I 've come up against, and maybe they did n't fee' any particular interest in me.    I did n't cut much shine as a ladies' man, but, I reckon now, it 's only because the right one had n't happened along.   She is here now, though, all right, and I knew it the very first time I set eyes on her.   Oh, you roped and tied me all right the first throw.   Maybe I did get you and that half-sister mixed up a bit, but just the same you were the one I really wanted.   Hope 's all right; she 's a mighty fine girl, but you are the one for me, Christie.   Could you — could you care for such a duffer as I am? "

Her lips were smiling and so were her eyes, but it was a pleading smile.

" I — I don't think it would be so very hard," she admitted, " not if you really wanted me to."

" You know what I mean — that I love you,— wish you to be my wife? "

" I supposed that was it — that — that you wanted me."

" Yes, and — and you will love me? "

Her head drooped slowly, so slowly he did not realize the significance of the action, until her lips touched his hand.

"I do," she said; "you are the best man in the world."

Fairbain could not move, could not seem to realize what it all meant. The outcome had been so sudden, so surprising, that all power of expression deserted him. In bewilderment he lifted her face, and looked into her eyes. Perhaps she realized — with the swift intuition of a clever woman — the man's perplexity, for instantly she led his mind to other things.

"But let us not talk of ourselves any more, to-night. There is so much I wish to know; so much that ought to be done." She sprang to her feet. "Why, it is almost shameful for us to stay here, selfishly happy, while others are in such trouble. Have they discovered Hope?"

"No; we scoured the whole town and found no trace. Now they are outside on the prairie, but there can be little chance of their picking up a trail before daylight."

"And Hawley?"

"He has vanished also; without doubt they are to-gether. What do you suppose he can want of her? How do you imagine he ever got her to go with him? She is n't that sort of a girl."

She shook her head, shivering a little.

" He must have mistaken her for me — perhaps has not even yet discovered his mistake. But what it all means, or how he gained her consent to go with him, I cannot conceive."

She stood with hands clasped, staring out the window.

" There is a little light showing already," she exclaimed, pointing. " See, yonder. Oh, I trust they will find her alive, and unhurt. That man, I believe, is capable of any crime. But could n't you be of some help? Why should you remain here with me? I am in no danger."

" You really wish me to go, Christie? "

" Not that way — not that way," and she turned impulsively, with hands outstretched. " Of course I want you here with me, but I want you to help bring Hope back."

He drew her to him, supremely happy now, every feeling of embarrassment lost in complete certainty of possession.

" And I will," he said solemnly. " Wherever they may have gone I shall follow. I am going now, dear, and when I come back you 'll be glad to see me? "

" Shall I? " her eyes uplifted to his own, and swimming in tears. " I will be the happiest girl in all the world, I reckon. Oh, what a night this has been!

What a wonderful night! It has given me a name, a mother, and the man I love."

He kissed her, not in passion, but in simple tenderness, and as he turned away she sank upon her knees at the window, with head bowed upon the sill. At the door he paused, and looked back, and she turned, and smiled at him. Then he went out, and she knelt there silently, gazing forth into the dawn, her eyes blurred with tears — facing a new day, and a new life.

# CHAPTER XXXIII

## FOLLOWING THE TRAIL

THE withdrawal of the sheriff merely stimulated Keith to greater activity. It was clearly evident the fugitives were endeavoring with all rapidity possible to get beyond where the hand of law could reach them — their trail striking directly across the plains into the barren southwest was proof of this purpose. Yet it was scarcely likely they would proceed very far in that direction, as such a course would bring them straight into the heart of the Indian country, into greater danger than that from which they fled. Keith felt no doubt that Hawley intended making for Carson City, where he could securely hide the girl, and where he possessed friends to rally to his defence, even an influence over the officers of the law. The one thing which puzzled him most was the man's object in attempting so desperate a venture. Did he know his prisoner was Hope Waite? or did he still suppose he was running off with Christie Maclaire? Could some rumor of Waite's appeal to the courts have reached the gambler, frightened him, and caused him to at-

tempt this desperate effort at escape? and did he bear
Miss Maclaire with him, hoping thus to keep her
safely concealed until he was better prepared to come
out in open fight? If this was the actual state of
affairs then it would account for much otherwise hard
to explain. The actress would probably not have been
missed, or, at least, seriously sought after, until she
failed to appear at the theatre the following evening.
This delay would give the fugitives a start of twenty
hours, or even more, and practically assure their safety.
Besides, in the light of Waite's application to the sheriff
for assistance, it was comparatively easy to conceive of a valid reason why Hawley should vanish,
and desire, likewise, to take Miss Maclaire with him.
But there was no apparent occasion for his forcible
abduction of Hope. Of course, he might have done
so from a suddenly aroused fit of anger at some discovery the girl had made, yet everything pointed rather
to a deliberate plan. Both horses and men were
certainly waiting there under orders, Hawley's ad-
herents in charge, and every arrangement perfected
in advance. Clearly enough, the gambler had planned
it all out before he ever went to the Trocadero —
no doubt the completion of these final arrangements
was what delayed his appearance at the hotel. If this
was all true, then it must have been Christie, and not

Hope, he purposed bearing away with him, and the latter was merely a victim of her masquerade.

What would result when the man discovered his mistake? Such a discovery could not be delayed long, although the girl was quick-witted, and would surely realize that her personal safety depended upon keeping up the deception to the last possible moment. Yet the discovery must finally occur, and there was no guessing what form Hawley's rage would assume when he found himself baffled, and all his plans for a fortune overturned. Keith fully realized Hope's peril, and his own helplessness to serve her in this emergency was agony. As they hurried back to the town, he briefly reviewed these conclusions with Waite and Fairbain, all alike agreeing there was nothing remaining for them to do except to take up the trail. The fugitives had already gained too great an advantage to be overhauled, but they might be traced to whatever point they were heading for. In spite of the start being so far to the west, Keith was firmly convinced that their destination would prove to be Carson City.

Procuring horses at the corral, their forces augmented by two volunteers — both men of experience — Keith, Waite, Fairbain, and Neb departed without delay, not even pausing to eat but taking the necessary food with them.  The sun had barely risen when they took up the trail, Keith, and a man named Bristoe, slightly in advance, their keen eyes marking every slight sign left for guidance across the bare plain.  It was a comparatively easy trail to follow, leading directly into the southwest, the pony tracks cutting into the sod as though the reckless riders had bunched together, their horses trotting rapidly.  Evidently no attempt had been made at concealment, and this served to convince the pursuers that Hawley still believed his captive to be Miss Maclaire, and that her disappearance would not be suspected until after nightfall.  In that case the trail could not be discovered before the following morning, and with such a start, pursuit would be useless.  Tireless, steadily, scarcely speaking except upon the business in hand, the pursuers pressed forward at an easy trot, Keith, in spite of intense anxiety, with the remembrance of old cavalry days to guide him, insisting upon sparing the horses as much as possible.  This was to be a stern chase and a long one, and it was impossible to tell when they could procure remounts.  The constant swerving of the trail westward seemed to shatter his earlier theory, and, brought him greater uneasiness.  Finally he spoke of it to the old plainsman beside him.

"What do suppose those fellows are heading so

Tireless, steadily, scarcely speaking, the pursuers pressed forward at
an easy trot

far west for, Ben? They are taking a big risk of running into hostiles."

"Oh, I don't know," returned the other gravely, lifting his eyes to the far-off sky line. "I reckon from the news thet come in last night from Hays, thar ain't no Injuns a rangin' thet way jist now. They're too blame busy out on the Arickaree. Maybe them fellers heerd the same story, an' thet's what makes 'em so bold."

"What story? I've heard nothing."

"Why, it's like this, Cap," drawling out the words, "leastways, thet's how it come inter Sheridan; 'Sandy' Forsythe an' his outfit, mostly plainsmen, started a while ago across Solomon River an' down Beaver Crick, headin' fer Fort Wallace. Over on the Arickaree, the whole damned Injun outfit jumped 'em. From all I heerd, thar must a bin nigh onto three thousan' o' the varmints, droppin' on 'em all at oncet, hell-bent-fer-election, with ol' Roman Nose a leadin' 'em. It was shore a good fight, fer the scouts got onto an island an' stopped the bucks. Two of the fellers got through to Wallace yist'day, an' a courier brought the news in ter Hays. The Injuns had them boys cooped up thar fer eight days before them fellers got out, an' I reckon it'll be two or three days more 'fore the nigger sogers they sent out ter help ever git thar.

So thar won't be no Injuns 'long this route we're travellin', fer the whole kit an' caboodle are up thar yit after ' Sandy.' "

" And you suppose Hawley knew about this? "

" Why not, Cap? He was hangin' 'round till after ten o'clock las' night, an' it was all over town by then. 'Tain't likely he's got an outfit 'long with him thet's lost any Injuns. I don't know whar they're bound, no mor'n you do, but I reckon they're reasonably sure they've got a clar road."

They pulled up on the banks of a small stream to water their horses, and ate hastily. The trail led directly across, and with only the slightest possible delay they forded the shallow water, and mounted the opposite bank. A hundred yards farther on, Bristoe reined up suddenly, pointing down at the trail.

" One hoss left the bunch here," he declared positively. Keith swung himself out of the saddle, and bent over to study the tracks. There was no doubting the evidence — a single horse — the only one shod in the bunch — with a rider on its back, judging from the deep imprint of the hoofs, had swerved sharply to the left of the main body, heading directly into the southeast. The plainsman ran forward for a hundred yards to assure himself the man had not circled back;

at that point the animal had been spurred into a lope. Keith rejoined the others.

"Must have been about daylight they reached here," he said, picking up his dangling rein, and looking into the questioning faces about him. "The fellow that rode out yonder alone was heading straight toward Carson City. He is going for fresh horses, I figure it, and will rejoin the bunch some place down on the Arkansas. The others intend to keep farther west, where they won't be seen. What do you say, Ben?"

"Thet's the way it looms up ter me, Cap; most likely 't was the boss himself."

"Well, whoever it was, the girl is still with the others, and their trail is the easiest to follow. We'll keep after them."

They pushed on hour after hour, as long as daylight lasted or they could perceive the faintest trace to follow. Already half-convinced that he knew the ultimate destination of the fugitives, Keith yet dare not venture on pressing forward during the night, thus possibly losing the trail and being compelled to retrace their steps. It was better to proceed slow and sure. Besides, judging from the condition of their own horses, the pursued would be compelled to halt somewhere to rest their stock also. Their trail even re-

vealed the fact that they were already travelling far
less rapidly than at first, although evidently making
every effort to cover the greatest possible distance before stopping.  Just as the dusk shut in close about
them they rode down into the valley of Shawnee Fork,
and discovered signs of a recent camp at the edge
of the stream.  Here, apparently, judging from the
camp-fire ashes, and the trampled grass along the
Fork, the party must have halted for several hours.
By lighting matches Keith and Bristoe discerned where
some among them had laid down to sleep, and, through
various signs, decided they must have again departed
some five or six hours previous, one of their horses
limping as if lame.  The tired pursuers went into camp
at the same spot, but without venturing to light any fire,
merely snatching a cold bite, and dropping off to sleep
with heads pillowed upon their saddles.

They were upon the trail again with the first dimness of .the gray dawn, wading the waters of the
Fork, and striking forth across the dull level of brown
prairie and white alkali toward the Arkansas.  They
saw nothing all day moving in that wide vista about
them, but rode steadily, scarcely exchanging a word,
determined, grim, never swerving a yard from
the faint trail.  The pursued were moving slower,
hampered, no doubt, by their lame horse, but were still

well in advance. Moreover, the strain of the saddle was already beginning to tell severely on Waite, weakened somewhat by years, and the pursuers were compelled to halt oftener on his account. The end of the second day found them approaching the broken land bordering the Arkansas valley, and just before nightfall they picked up a lame horse, evidently discarded by the party ahead.

By this time Keith had reached a definite decision as to his course. If the fugitives received a fresh relay of horses down there somewhere, and crossed the Arkansas, he felt positively sure as to their destination. But it would be useless pushing on after them in the present shape of his party — their horses worn out, and Waite reeling giddily in the saddle. If Hawley's outfit crossed the upper ford, toward which they were evidently heading, and struck through the sand hills, then they were making for the refuge of that lone cabin on Salt Fork. Should this prove true, then it was probable the gambler had not even yet discovered the identity of Hope, for if he had, he would scarcely venture upon taking her there, knowing that Keith would naturally suspect the spot. But Keith would not be likely to personally take up the trail in search for Christie Maclaire. It must have been Hawley then who had left the party and ridden east, and up to that time he had not found out his mistake. Yet if he brought out the fresh animals the chances were that Hope's identity would be revealed. Bristoe, who had turned aside to examine the straying horse, came trotting up.

" Belonged to their outfit all right, Cap," he reported, " carries the double cross brand and that shebang is upon the Smoky; saddle galls still bleeding."

Waite was now suffering so acutely they were obliged to halt before gaining sight of the river, finding, fortunately, a water-hole fed by a spring. As soon as the sick man could be made comfortable, Keith gave to the others his conclusions, and listened to what they had to say. Bristoe favored clinging to the trail even though they must travel slowly, but Fairbain insisted that Waite must be taken to some town where he could be given necessary care. Keith finally decided the matter.

" None can be more anxious to reach those fellows than I am," he declared, " but I know that country out south, and we 'll never get through to the Salt Fork without fresh horses. Besides, as the doctor says, we 've got to take care of Waite. If we find things as I expect we 'll ride for Carson City, and reoutfit there. What 's more, we won't lose much time

— it 's a shorter ride from there to the cabin than from here."

By morning the General was able to sit his saddle again, and leaving him with Neb to follow slowly, the others spurred forward, discovered an outlet through the bluff into the valley, and crossed the Santa Fé Trail. It was not easy to discover where those in advance had passed this point, but they found evidence of a late camp in a little grove of cottonwoods beside the river. There were traces of two trails leading to the spot, one being that of the same five horses they had been following so long, the other not so easily read, as it had been traversed in both directions, the different hoof marks obliterating each other. Bristoe, creeping about on hands and knees, studied the signs with the eyes of an Indian.

"You kin see the diff'rence yere whar the ground is soft, Cap," he said, pointing to some tracks plainer than the others. "This yere hoss had a rider, but the rest of 'em was led; thet 's why they 've bungled up ther trail so. An' it wa'n't ther same bunch thet went back east what come from thar — see thet split hoof! thar ain't no split hoof p'inting ther other way — but yere is the mark of the critter thet puts her foot down so fur outside thet we 've been a trailin' from Sheridan, an' she's p'inting east, an' being led.   Now, let's see whar the bunch went from yere with thet split hoof."

This was not so easily accomplished owing to the nature of the ground, but at last the searchers stumbled onto tracks close in under the bank, and one of these revealed the split hoof.

"That makes it clear, Ben," exclaimed Keith, decidedly, staring out across the river at the white sand-hills.   "They have kept in the edge of the water, making for the ford, which is yonder at the bend. They are out in the sand desert by this time riding for the Salt Fork.   Whoever he was, the fellow brought them five horses, and the five old ones were taken east again on the trail.   The girl is still with the party, and we'll go into Carson City and reoutfit."

# CHAPTER XXXIV

## AGAIN AT THE CABIN

THEY were two weary days reaching Carson City, travelling along the open trail yet meeting with no one, not even a mail coach passing them. Evidently the Indians were so troublesome as to interrupt all traffic with Santa Fé and the more western forts. The slowness of their progress was on account of the General, whose condition became worse in spite of Fairbain's assiduous attentions. With no medicine the doctor could do but little to relieve the sufferings of the older man, although he declared that his illness was not a serious one, and would yield quickly to proper medical treatment. They constructed a rude travois from limbs of the cottonwood, and securely strapped him thereon, one man leading the horse, while the doctor tramped behind.

Keith, fretting more and more over this necessary delay, and now obsessed with the thought that Hawley must have rejoined his party on the Arkansas and gone south with them, finally broke away from the others and rode ahead, to gather together the necessary horses and supplies in advance of their arrival. He could not drive from his mind the remembrance of the gambler's attempted familiarity with Hope, when he had her, as he then supposed, safe in his power once before in that lonely cabin on the Salt Fork. Now, angry with baffled ambition, and a victim of her trickery, there was no guessing to what extremes the desperado might resort. The possibilities of such a situation made the slightest delay in rescue an agony almost unbearable. Reaching Carson City, and perfectly reckless as to his own safety there from arrest, the plainsman lost no time in perfecting arrangements for pushing forward. Horses and provisions were procured, and he very fortunately discovered in town two cowboys belonging to the " Bar X " outfit, their work there accomplished and about ready to return to the ranch on the Canadian, who gladly allied themselves with his party, looking forward to the possibilities of a fight with keen anticipation. Keith was more than ever delighted with adding these to his outfit, when, on the final arrival of the others, the extra man brought from Sheridan announced that he had had enough, and was going to remain there. No efforts made revealed any knowledge of Hawley's presence in Carson City; either he had not been there, or else his friends were very carefully concealing the fact.

The utter absence of any trace, however, led Keith to believe that the gambler had gone elsewhere — probably to Fort Larned — for his new outfit, and this belief left him more fully convinced than ever of the fellow's efforts to conceal his trail.

The party escorting Waite reached the town in the evening, and in the following gray dawn, the adventurers forded the river, and mounted on fresh horses and fully equipped, headed forth into the sand hills. The little company now consisted of Keith, Fairbain, who, in spite of his rotundity of form had proven himself hard and fit, Neb, having charge of the single packhorse, the scout Bristoe, and the two cowboys of the " Bar X," rough, wiry fellows, accustomed to exposure and peril. It was emphatically a fighting outfit, and to be trusted in emergency.

They followed the cattle trail south toward the Salt Fork, as this course would afford them a camp at the only water-hole in all that wide desert lying between. With this certainty of water, they ventured to press their animals to swifter pace, although the sand made travelling heavy, and the trail itself was scarcely discernible. It was a hard, wearisome ride, hour after hour through the same dull, dreary landscape of desolation, the hot, remorseless sun beating down upon them, reflecting up into their blistered faces from the hot surface of sand. There was scarcely a breath of air, and the bodies of men and horses were bathed in perspiration. Not a cloud hung in the blue sky; no wing of a bird broke the monotony of distance, no living animal crept across the blazing surface of the desert. Occasionally a distant mirage attracted the eye, making the dead reality even more horrible by its semblance to water, yet never tempting them to stray aside. After the first mile conversation ceased, the men riding grimly, silently forward, intent only on covering all the distance possible. Late that night they camped at the water-hole, sleeping as best they could, scourged by the chill wind which swept over them and lashed grit into exposed faces. With the first gray of dawn they swung stiffened forms into the saddles and rode on, straight as the crow flies, for the Salt Fork. They attained that stream at sundown, gray with sand dust, their faces streaked from perspiration, feeling as though the sun rays had burned their brains, with horses fairly reeling under them. According to Keith's calculation this cattle-ford must be fully ten miles below where the cabin sought was situated; two hours' rest, with water and food, would put both horses and men again in condition, and the travelling was easier along the banks of the Fork. With this in mind, cinches were loosened, the animals turned out to graze, and the men, snatching a hasty bite, flung themselves wearily on the ground.

All but Fairbain were asleep when Keith aroused them once more, a little before nine, unable in his impatience to brook longer delay. Within ten minutes horses were saddled, weapons looked to carefully, and the little party began their advance through the darkness, moving cautiously over the uneven ground, assisted greatly by the bright desert stars gleaming down upon them from the cloudless sky overhead. The distance proved somewhat less than had been anticipated, and Keith's watch was not yet at eleven, when his eyes revealed the fact that they had reached the near vicinity of the lonely island on which the cabin stood. Reining in his horse sharply, he swung to the ground, the others instantly following his example, realizing they had reached the end of the route. Hands instinctively loosened revolvers in readiness for action, the younger of the " Bar X " men whistling softly in an effort to appear unconcerned. Keith, with a gesture, gathered them more closely about him.

" If Hawley is here himself," he said quietly, watching their faces in the starlight, " he will certainly have a guard set, and there may be one anyhow. We can't afford to take chances, for there will be five men, at least, on the island, and possibly several more. If they are looking for trouble they will naturally expect it to come from the north — consequently we 'll make our attack from the opposite direction, and creep in on them under the shadow of the corral.   The first thing I want to do is to locate Miss Waite so she will be in no danger of getting hurt in the *mêlée*.   You boys hold your fire, until I let loose or give the word.   Now, Doctor, I want you and Neb to creep up this bank until you are directly opposite the cabin — he 'll know the spot — and lie there out of sight until we begin the shooting.  Then both sail in as fast as you can.   I 'll take Bristoe and you two ' Bar X ' men along with me, and when we turn loose with our shooting irons you can all reckon the fight is on.   Any of you got questions to ask? "

No one said anything, the silence accented by the desert wind howling mournfully in the branches of a near-by cottonwood.

" All right then, boys, don't get excited and go off half cocked; be easy on your trigger fingers.   Come along, you fellows who are travelling with me."

The four crossed the stream, wading to their waists in the water, their horses left bunched on the south bank, and finally crawled out into a bunch of mesquite. As they crept along through the darkness, whatever doubts Keith might have previously felt regarding the presence on the island of the party sought, were dissipated by the unmistakable noise made by numerous horses in the corral. Slowly, testing each step as they advanced, so no sound should betray them, the four men reached the shelter of the stockade. The older of the " Bar X " men lifted himself by his hands, and peered cautiously over.

" Eight hosses in thar," he announced soberly; then turned to Keith. " Say, Jack, what do you figure this shebang to be, anyhow? You don't reckon it 's old Sanchez's outfit, do yer? "

" Likely as not, Joe, though I never saw him around here."

Joe filled his cheek with tobacco, staring about through the darkness.

" Wall, if that ol' cuss is yere now we'uns is sure in fer a fight," he commented positively.

They rounded the corral fence on hands and knees, crawled into a bunch of bushes somewhat to the rear of the silent, desolate-appearing cabin, and lay down flat behind a pile of saddles, from which position they could plainly discern the rear door. There was no movement, no evidence anywhere that a living soul was about the place. Keith could barely distinguish that it was Bristoe lying next to him.

"Had their camp over there in the corner of the corral when I was here before," he said in a whisper. "Where do you suppose they can be now?"

The wary scout lifted his head, sniffing into the darkness like a pointer dog.

"West o' ther cabin thar, out o' ther wind, most likely. I smell tobacco."

Even as the words left his lips a man came sauntering slowly around the eastern corner, his outlines barely visible, but the red glow of a pipe bowl showing plainly. He stopped, directly facing them, yawning sleepily, and then turned the other corner. Another moment, and they distinctly heard a voice:

"Hustle up thar now, Manuel, an' turn out; it's your watch; wake up, damn yer — maybe that 'll bring yer ter life."

The remedy applied to the sleeper must have been efficacious, as, an instant later, another figure slouched into view, the new arrival rubbing his eyes with one hand, the other clutching a short-barrelled gun. From the high peak of his hat it was evident this new guard was a Mexican. He walked to the corner, glanced along the east side wall toward the front of the cabin, and then, apparently satisfied the coast was clear, started toward the stream, shuffling along within a foot of where Keith lay flat on the ground. A moment later the men heard him splashing softly in the water, and Keith rolled over, his lips at Bristoe's ear.

" Slip down there, Ben," he whispered, " and quiet that fellow. I 'll find out how many are on the west side. Do the job without any noise."

He waited until the scout had disappeared like a snake, not even a rustling leaf telling of his passage, and then silently crept forward himself, yet with less caution, until he was able to peer about the corner of the cabin and dimly distinguish the blanketed forms of several men lying close in against the side wall. They rested so nearly together it was difficult to separate them in that darkness, stars giving the only light, but he finally determined their number at five. Five; the Mexican would make six, and there would surely be another guard posted out in the front — seven. But there were eight horses down there in the corral. Then the eighth man — Hawley, without doubt — must be in the cabin. At the thought Keith's teeth clinched, and he had to struggle to control his passion. But no; that would never do; he must discover first exactly where the girl was located; after that they would attend to the curs. Before creeping back to the others, he made quick examination along the rear of the cabin, but could find no visible point of weakness. He tried to recall from memory the nature of the lock on that back door, but could remember nothing except an ordinary wooden latch. If he could insert a knife into the crack that might very easily be dislodged. He drew his hunting knife for the attempt, and, first glancing about, perceived a man creeping toward him. It proved to be Bristoe.

" Fixed the greaser all right, cap, and I reckon he 'll be quiet for an hour or two. Look whar he slashed me; struck a pack o' playin' keerds, er I 'd a got my ticket." The front of his blouse was cut wide open, and Keith thought he perceived a stain of blood.

" Pricked you as it was, did n't he ? "

" Opened the skin. Thought the cuss had give up, an' got careless. What 's 'round to the west ? "

Keith's lips closed, his hand shutting hard on the knife.

" Five, and another out in front; that leaves the eighth man inside. Bring our fellows up closer, and post them where they can cover those fellows asleep, while I make an effort at breaking in here."

Bristoe crawled back like a snail, and confident the others would do their part, Keith thrust his knife blade deep into the narrow crack, and began probing after the latch. In spite of all caution this effort caused a slight noise, and suddenly he started back, at the sound of a woman's voice:

"What do you want? I am armed, and will fire through the door if you do not go away!"

His heart leaping with exultation, Keith put his lips close to the crack.

"Hope," he exclaimed as loudly as he dared. "This is Keith; open the door."

He could hear a little smothered cry break from her lips, and then the sound of a bar being hastily removed. An instant, and the door opened silently, just wide enough to permit her slender figure to slip through. She grasped him with her hands, turning his face to the light of the stars, and he could feel her form tremble.

"Oh, I knew you would come! I knew you would come!" she sobbed, the words barely audible.

The man's lips set firmly, yet he held her close to him, begging her not to break down now.

"It's all right, little girl," he said pleadingly, "we've got you safe, but there is a fight to be attended to. Come with me; I must ask you a question or two."

He drew her back into the fringe of bushes, placing her safely behind the stack of saddles. She was not crying any more, just clinging to him, as though she could never again bear to let him go.

"Oh, Jack, it is so good just to feel you near again."

"Yes, dear," soothingly, "and it is good to hear

you say Jack, but tell me one thing — is any one else in the cabin? Is Hawley here?"

"No, no! He left us early the first morning. I have n't either seen or heard of him since. The men have left me alone since we got here; I have had the cabin all to myself until to-night. I have not suffered, only mentally — from dread of what they intended doing with me — until to-night. Three men rode in here just before sundown — two Mexicans and an Indian. One of them was an awful looking old man, with a scar on his cheek, and a face that made me shudder. He did n't see me, but I saw him through the window, and he had such strange eyes. All the men acted as though they were afraid of him, and I heard him say he did n't care what Hawley's orders were, he was going to sleep inside; if the girl did n't like it she could take the other room. I did n't know what to do — oh, I was so afraid of him; but what he said gave me an idea, and I went into the back room, and put up a bar across the door. When he came in he tried the door; then he spoke through it, but I never answered; and finally he lay down and went to sleep. I sat there in the dark so long, and when I heard you — I — I thought it must be some of the others."

He stroked her hair, whispering words of encouragement.

" That is all done with now, Hope, and we 'll have those fellows at our mercy in another half-hour. But I must go now to the boys; lie down here behind these saddles, and don't move until I come for you. I can trust you to remain right here? "

" Yes." He was bending over, and her eyes were upon his face. Suddenly, obeying an irresistible impulse, he clasped her to him, and their lips met.

" Sweetheart," he whispered softly.

He could not hear her answer, but her arms were about his neck.

# CHAPTER XXXV

## THE CABIN TAKEN

HIS heart beating with new happiness, yet conscious of the stern duty still confronting him, Keith joined the others, giving them, in a whisper, a hurried account of Hope's release from the cabin, and of what she had to report.

" It 's old Juan Sanchez in the front room, boys," he added soberly, " and there is ten thousand dollars reward out for him, dead or alive."

Joe of the " Bar X " drew in his breath sharply.

" It'll sure be dead then," he muttered, " that cuss will never be got no other way."

They went at it in the grim silent manner of the West, wasting little time, feeling no mercy. One by one the unconscious sleepers were aroused, each waking to find a steel barrel pressing against his forehead, and to hear a stern voice say ominously, " Not a move, Johnny; yes, that 's a gun; now get up quietly, and step out here." Resistance was useless, and the five, rendered weaponless, were herded back toward the corral. They all belonged to Hawley's outfit; one, a black-whiskered surly brute Bristoe remembered having seen in Sheridan. There was no time to deal with them then, and a " Bar X " man was placed on guard, with orders to shoot at the slightest suspicious movement.

The Indian, then, would be guarding the front of the house, and Sanchez sleeping inside. Well, the former could be left alone; his chance of escape would be small enough with Fairbain and Neb on the opposite bank. Old Sanchez was the villain they wanted — dead or alive. With this in view, and anxious to make a quick job of it, the three entered the back room, and, revolvers in hand, groped their way across to the connecting door. As Hope had described, this had been securely fastened by a stout wooden bar. Bristoe forced it from the sockets, not without some slight noise, and Keith, crouching down at one side, lifted the latch.

" Keep down low, boys," he cautioned, " where he can't hit you."

With one quick push he flung the door wide open, and a red flash lit the room. There were two sharp reports, the bullets crashing into the wall behind them, the sudden blaze of flame revealing the front door open, and within it the black outline of a man's figure. Two of the men fired in instant response, leaping recklessly forward, but were as quickly left blind in the darkness, the outer door slammed in their faces. Outside there was a snarl of rage, another shot, a fierce curse in Spanish; then Keith flung the door wide open, and leaped down the step. As he did so he struck a body, and fell forward, his revolver knocked from his hand. Rising to his knees, the dim light of the stars revealed a man already half across the stream. Suddenly two sparks of fire leaped forth from the blackness of the opposite bank; the man flung up his hand, staggered, then went stumbling up the stream, knee deep in water. He made a dozen yards, reeling as though drunk, and fell forward, face down across a spit of sand. Keith stared out at the black, motionless shape, felt along the ground for his lost gun, and arose to his feet. Bristoe had turned over the dead body at the foot of the steps, and was peering down into the upturned face.

" It 's the Indian," he said grimly, " Sanchez must 'a' mistook him fer one of us, and shot the poor devil."

" And Sanchez himself is out yonder on that sandspit," and Keith pointed; then lifted his voice to make it carry across the stream. " Come on over, Doctor, you and Neb. We 've got the gang. Bring that body out there along with you."

The " Bar X " man waded out to help, and the three together laid the dead Mexican outlaw on the bank, beside the Indian he had shot down in his effort to escape. Keith stood for a moment bending low to look curiously into the dead face — wrinkled, scarred, still featuring cruelty, the thin lips drawn back in a snarl. What scenes of horror those eyes had gazed upon during fifty years of crime; what suffering of men, women, children; what deeds of rapine; what examples of merciless hate. Juan Sanchez! — the very sound of the name made the blood run cold. "Dead or alive!" Well, they had him at last — dead; and the plainsman shuddered, as he turned away.

Taking Fairbain with him, and hastily reviewing late occurrences to him, Keith crossed over to the corral, realizing that their work — his work — was not wholly done until Hawley had been located. With this quest in mind he strode straight to the black-bearded giant who had guarded Hope from Sheridan.

"What is your name?" he asked sharply.

The man looked up scowling.

"Hatchett," he answered gruffly.

"Well, Hatchett, I am going to ask you a question or two, and advise you to reply just about as straight as you know how. I am in no mood to-night for any foolishness. Where is 'Black Bart' Hawley?"

"How in hell should I know?"

"You do know, just the same. Perhaps not to an

inch, or a mile, but you know near enough where he is, and where he has been since you left Sheridan."

" If I do, I 'm damned if I 'll tell you."

" No? Well now, Hatchett, listen to me," and Keith's voice had in it the click of a steel trap. " You 'll either answer, and answer straight, or we 'll hang you to that cottonwood in about five minutes. If you want a chance for your miserable life you answer me. We have our way of treating your kind out in this country. Sit up, you brute! Now where did Hawley go after he left you? "

" To Fort Larned."

" After those fresh horses? "

" Yes."

" He did n't bring them to you; I know that. Where has he been since? "

" Topeky and Leavenworth."

" How do you know? "

" He writ me a note the boss herder brought."

" Hand it over."

Keith took the dirty slip of paper the man reluctantly extracted from his belt, and Fairbain lit matches while he ran his eyes hastily over the lines. As he ended he crushed the paper between his fingers, and walked away to the end of the corral. He wanted to be alone, to think, to decide definitely upon what he

ought to do.  Hawley, according to the schedule just
read, must have left Larned alone early the day before; this night he would be camped at the water-hole;
with daybreak he expected to resume his lonely journey
across the desert to the Salt Fork.  For years Keith
had lived a primitive life, and in some ways his thought
had grown primitive.  His code of honor was that of
the border, tinged by that of the South before the war.
The antagonism existing between him and this gambler
was personal, private, deadly — not an affair for any
others — outsiders — to meddle with.  He could wait
here, and permit Hawley to be made captive; could
watch him ride unsuspectingly into the power of these
armed men, and then turn him over to the law to be
dealt with.  The very thought nauseated him.  That
would be a coward's act, leaving a stain never to be
eradicated.  No, he must meet this as became a man,
and now, now before Hope so much as dreamed of his
purpose — aye, and before he spoke another word of
love to Hope.  He wheeled about fully decided on his
course, his duty, and met Fairbain face to face.

"Jack," the latter said earnestly, "I read the note
over your shoulder, and of course I know what you
mean to do.  A Southern gentleman could not choose
otherwise.  But I 've come here to beg you to let me
have the chance."

" You? " surprised and curious. " What greater claim on that fellow's life have you than I ? "

The pudgy hands of the doctor grasped the plainsman's shoulders.

" It 's for Christie," he explained brokenly. " She was the one he tried to run away with. You — you know how I feel."

" Sure, I know," shaking the other off, yet not roughly. " But it happened to be Miss Waite he took, and so this is my job, Fairbain. Besides, I 've got another score to settle with him."

He wasted little time upon preparations,— a few brief words of instruction to Bristoe; a request to the doctor not to leave Hope alone; the extracting of a promise from the two " Bar X " men to return to Larned with the prisoners. Then he roped the best horse in the corral, saddled and bridled him, and went into the cabin. She had a light burning, and met him at the door.

" I thought you would never come, but they told me you were unhurt."

" Not a scratch, little girl; we have been a lucky bunch. But I have had a great deal to look after. Now I shall be obliged to ride ahead as far as the waterhole, and let you come on with the others a little later, after you get breakfast. You can spare me a few hours, can't you? "

His tone was full of good humor, and his lips smiling, yet somehow she felt her heart sink, an inexplicable fear finding expression in her eyes.

" But — but why do you need to go? Could n't some of the others? "

" There is a reason which I will explain later," he said, more gravely. " Surely you can trust me, Hope, and feel that I am only doing what it seems absolutely necessary for me to do? " He bent down, and kissed her. " It will be only for a few hours, and no cause for worry. Good-bye now, until we meet to-night at the water-hole."

The east was gray with coming daylight as he rode plashing across the stream and up the opposite bank. She watched him, rubbing the blinding mist from her eyes, until horse and man became a mere dark speck, finally fading away completely into the dull plain of the desert.

# CHAPTER XXXVI

## THE DUEL IN THE DESERT

KEITH rode straight forward into the sandy desolation, spurring his horse into a swift trot. After one glance backward as they clambered up the steep bank, a glance which revealed Hope's slender form in the cabin door, his eyes never turned again that way. He had a man's stern work to do out yonder, and his purpose could not be swerved, his firmness of hand and keenness of eye affected, by any thought of her. His lips compressed, his fingers gripping the rein, he drove all regretful memory from his mind, until every nerve within him throbbed in unison with his present purpose. He was right; he knew he was right. It was not hate, not even revenge, which had sent him forth, leaving love behind, but honor — the honor of the South, and of the frontier, of his ancestry and his training — honor that drove him now to meet Hawley face to face, man to man, to settle the feud between them for all time. And he rode smiling, gladly, as to a tryst, now that he was at last alone, free in the desert.

The hours passed, the sun rising higher in the blazing blue of the sky; the horse, wearied by the constant pull of the sand, had long since slowed down to a walk; the last dim blur of the cottonwoods along the Fork had disappeared; and the rider swayed in the saddle, the dead lifelessness of sky and desert dulling his brain. Yet he had not forgotten his errand — rousing constantly from lethargy to sweep his shaded eyes about the rounded horizon, keenly marking the slightest shadow across the sands, taking advantage of every drift to give him wider viewpoint, rising in his stirrups to scan the leagues of desolation ahead. Twice he drew his revolver from out its sheath, tested it, and slipped in a fresh cartridge, returning the weapon more lightly to its place, the flap of the holster turned back and held open by his leg. The sun beat upon him like a ball of fire, the hot sand flinging the blaze back into his face. He pushed back the upper part of his shirt, and drank a swallow of tepid water from a canteen strapped behind the saddle. His eyes ached with the glare, until he saw fantastic red and yellow shapes dancing dizzily before him. The weariness of the long night pressed upon his eye-balls; he felt the strain of the past hours, the lack of food, the need of rest. His head nodded, and he brought himself to life again with a jerk and a muttered word, staring out into the dim, formless distance. Lord, if there was only something moving; something he could concentrate his attention upon; something to rest the straining eyes!

But there was nothing, absolutely nothing — just that seemingly endless stretch of sand, circled by the blazing sky, the wind sweeping its surface soundless, and hot, as though from the pits of hell; no stir, no motion, no movement of anything animate or inanimate to break the awful monotony. Death! it was death everywhere! his aching eyes rested on nothing but what was typical of death. Even the heat waves seemed fantastic, grotesque, assuming spectral forms, as though ghosts beckoned and danced in the haze, luring him on to become one of themselves. Keith was not a dreamer, nor one to yield easily to such brain fancies, but the mad delirium of loneliness gripped him, and he had to struggle back to sanity, beating his hands upon his breast to stir anew the sluggish circulation of his blood, and talking to the horse in strange feverishness.

With every step of advance the brooding silence seemed more profound, more deathlike. He got to marking the sand ridges, their slight variations giving play to the brain. Way off to the left was the mirage of a lake, apparently so real that he had to battle with himself to keep from turning aside. He dropped forward in the saddle, his head hanging low, so blinded by the incessant sun glare he could no longer bear the glitter of that horrible ocean of sand.   It was noon now — noon, and he had been riding steadily seven hours. The thought brought his blurred eyes again to the horizon.   Where could he be, the man he sought in the heart of this solitude?   Surely he should be here by now, if he had left the water-hole at dawn.   Could he have gone the longer route, south to the Fork?   The possibility of such a thing seared through him like a hot iron, driving the dulness from his brain, the lethargy from his limbs.   God! no!   Fate could never play such a scurvy trick as that!   The man must have been delayed; had failed to leave camp early — somewhere ahead, yonder where the blue haze marked the union of sand and sky, he was surely coming, riding half dead, and drooping in the saddle.

Again Keith rose in his stirrups, rubbing the mist out of his eyes that he might see clearer, and stared ahead.   What was that away out yonder? a shadow? a spot dancing before his tortured vision? or a moving, living something which he actually saw?   He could not tell, he could not be sure, yet he straightened up expectantly, shading his eyes, and never losing sight of the object.   It moved, grew larger, darker, more real — yet how it crawled, crawled, crawled toward him.   It seemed as if the vague, shapeless thing would never take form, never stand out revealed against the sky so he could determine the truth. He had forgotten all else — the silent desert, the blazing sun, the burning wind — all his soul concentrated on that speck yonder. Suddenly it disappeared — a swale in the sand probably — and, when it rose into view again, he uttered a cry of joy — it was a horse and rider!

Little by little they drew nearer one another, two black specks in that vast ocean of sand, the only moving, living things under the brazen circle of the sky. Keith was ready now, his eyes bright, the cocked revolver gripped hard in his hand. The space between them narrowed, and Hawley saw him, caught a glimpse of the face under the broad hat brim, the burning eyes surveying him. With an oath he stopped his horse, dragging at his gun, surprised, dazed, yet instantly understanding. Keith also halted, and across the intervening desert the eyes of the two men met in grim defiance. The latter wet his dry lips, and spoke shortly:

" I reckon you know what this means, Hawley, and why I am here. We 're Southerners both of us, and we settle our own personal affairs. You 've got to fight me now, man to man."

The gambler glanced about him, and down at his

Across the intervening desert the eyes of the two men met
in grim defiance

horse.  If he thought of flight it was useless.  His lip curled with contempt.

"Damn your talking, Keith," he returned savagely. "Let's have it over with," and spurred his horse.  The gun of the other came up.

"Wait!" and Hawley paused, dragging at his rein. "One of us most likely is going to die here; perhaps both.  But if either survives he'll need a horse to get out of this alive.  Dismount; I'll do the same; step away so the horses are out of range, and then we'll fight it out — is that square?"

Without a word, his eyes gleaming with cunning hatred, the gambler swung down from his saddle onto the sand, his horse interposed between him and the other.  Keith did the same, his eyes peering across the back of his animal.

"Now," he said steadily, "when I count three drive your horse aside, and let go — are you ready?"

"Damn you — yes!"

"Then look out — one! two! three!"

The plainsman struck his horse with the quirt in his left hand, and sprang swiftly aside so as to clear the flank of the animal, his shooting arm flung out.  There was a flash of flame across Hawley's saddle, a sharp report, and Keith reeled backward, dropping to his knees, one hand clutching at the sand. Again Hawley fired, but the horse, startled by the double report, leaped aside, and the ball went wild. Keith wheeled about, steadying himself with his outstretched hand, and let drive, pressing the trigger, until, through the haze over his eyes, he saw Hawley go stumbling down, shooting wildly as he fell. The man never moved, and Keith endeavored to get up, his gun still held ready, the smoke circling about them. He had been shot treacherously, as a cowardly cur might shoot, and he could not clear his mind of the thought that this last act hid treachery also. But he could not raise himself, could not stand; red and black shadows danced before his eyes; he believed he saw the arm of the other move. Like a snake he crept forward, holding himself up with one hand, his head dizzily reeling, but his gun held steadily on that black, shapeless object lying on the sand. Then the revolver hand began to quiver, to shake, to make odd circles; he could n't see; it was all black, all nothingness. Suddenly he went down face first into the sand.

They both lay motionless, the thirsty sand drinking in their life blood, Hawley huddled up upon his left side, his hat still shading the glazing eyes, Keith lying flat, his face in the crook of an arm whose hand still gripped a revolver. There was a grim smile on his lips, as if, even as he pitched forward, he knew that, after he had been shot to death, he had gotten his man.    The riderless horses gazed at the two figures, and drifted away, slowly, fearfully, still held in mute subjection to their dead masters by dangling reins.    The sun blazed down from directly overhead, the heat waves rising and falling, the dead, desolate desert stretching to the sky. An hour, two hours passed.  The horses were now a hundred yards away, nose to nose; all else was changeless.    Then into the far northern sky there rose a black speck, growing larger and larger; others came from east and west, beating the air with widely outspread wings, great beaks stretched forward.    Out from their nests of foulness the desert scavengers were coming for their spoil.

# CHAPTER XXXVII

## AT THE WATER-HOLE

UP from the far, dim southwest they rode slowly, silently, wearied still by the exertions of the past night, and burned by the fierce rays of the desert sun. No wind of sufficient force had blown since Keith passed that way, and they could easily follow the hoof prints of his horse across the sand waste. Bristoe was ahead, hat brim drawn low, scanning the horizon line unceasingly. Somewhere out in the midst of that mystery was hidden tragedy, and he dreaded the knowledge of its truth. Behind him Fairbain and Hope rode together, their lips long since grown silent, the man ever glancing uneasily aside at her, the girl drooping slightly in the saddle, with pale face and heavy eyes. Five prisoners, lashed together, the binding ropes fastened to the pommels of the two " Bar X " men's saddles, were bunched together, and behind all came Neb, his black face glistening in the heat.

Suddenly Bristoe drew rein, and rose to his full length in the stirrups, shading his eyes from the sun's glare, as he stared ahead. Two motionless black

354

specks were visible — yet were they motionless? or was it the heat waves which seemed to yield them movement? He drove in his spurs, driving his startled horse to the summit of a low sand ridge, and again halted, gazing intently forward. He was not mistaken — they were horses. Knowing instantly what it meant — those riderless animals drifting derelict in the heart of the desert — his throat dry with fear, the scout wheeled, and spurred back to his party, quickly resolving on a course of action. Hawley and Keith had met; both had fallen, either dead or wounded. A moment's delay now might cost a life; he would need Fairbain, but he must keep the girl back, if possible. But could he? She straightened up in the saddle as he came spurring toward them; her eyes wide open, one hand clutching at her throat.

"Doctor," he called as soon as he was near enough, his horse circling, "thar is somethin' showin' out yonder I 'd like ter take a look at, an' I reckon you better go 'long. The nigger kin com' up ahead yere with Miss Waite."

She struck her horse, and he plunged forward, bringing her face to face with Bristoe.

"What is it? Tell me, what is it?"

"Nothin' but a loose hoss, Miss."

"A horse! here on the desert?" looking about, her

eyes dark with horror. " But how could that be? Could — could it be Captain Keith's ? "

Bristoe cast an appealing glance at Fairbain, mopping his face vigorously, not knowing what to say, and the other attempted to turn the tide.

" Not likely — not likely at all — no reason why it should be — probably just a stray horse — you stay back here, Miss Hope — Ben and I will find out, and let you know."

She looked at the two faces, realizing intuitively that they were concealing something.

" No, I 'm going," she cried, stifling a sob in her throat. " It would kill me to wait here."

She was off before either might raise hand or voice in protest, and they could only urge their horses in effort to overtake her, the three racing forward fetlock deep in sand. Mounted upon a swifter animal Fairbain forged ahead; he could see the two horses now plainly, their heads uplifted, their reins dangling. Without perceiving more he knew already what was waiting them there on the sand, and swore fiercely, spurring his horse mercilessly, forgetful of all else, even the girl, in his intense desire to reach and touch the bodies. He had begged to do this himself, to be privileged to seek this man Hawley, to kill him — but now he was the physician, with no other thought except a hope to save. Before his horse had even stopped he flung himself from the saddle, ran forward and dropped on his knees beside Keith, bending his ear to the chest, grasping the wrist in his fingers. As the others approached, he glanced up, no conception now of aught save his own professional work.

"Water, Bristoe," he exclaimed sharply, "Dash some brandy in it. Quick now. There, that's it; hold his head up — higher. Yes, you do it, Miss Hope; here, Ben, take this, and pry his teeth open — well, he got a swallow anyhow. Hold him just as he is — can you stand it? I've got to find where he was hit."

"Yes — yes," she answered, "don't — don't mind me."

He tore open the woolen shirt, soaked with blood already hardening, felt within with skilled fingers, his eyes keen, his lips muttering unconsciously.

"Quarter of an inch — quarter of an inch too high — scraped the lung — Lord, if I can only get it out — got to do it now — can't wait — here, Bristoe, that leather case on my saddle — run, damn you — we'll save him yet, girl — there, drop his head in your lap — yes, cry if you want to — only hold still — open the case, will you — down here, where I can reach it — now water — all our canteens — Hope, tear me off

a strip of your under-skirt — what am I going to do?
— extract the ball — got to do it — blood poison in
this sun."

She ripped her skirt, handing it to him without a
word; then dropped her white face in her hands, bending, with closed eyes, over the whiter face resting on
her lap, her lips trembling with the one prayer, " Oh,
God! Oh, God!" How long he was at it, or what he
did, she scarcely knew — she heard the splash of water;
caught the flash of the sun on the probe; felt the half
conscious shudder of the wounded man, whose head
was in her lap, the deft, quick movements of Fairbain,
and then —

" That's it — I've got it — missed the lung by a
hair — damn me I'm proud of that job — you're a
good girl."

She looked at him, scarce able to see, her eyes blinded
with tears.

" Will — will he live?   Oh, tell me! "

" Live!   Why shouldn't he? — nothing but a hole
to close up — nature 'll do that, with a bit of nursing
— here, now, don't you keel over — give me the rest
of that skirt."

He bandaged the wound, then glanced about suddenly.

" How 's the other fellow? "

" Dead," returned Bristoe, " shot through the heart."

" Thought so — have seen Keith shoot before — I wonder how the cuss ever managed to get him."

As he arose to his feet, his red face glistening with perspiration, and began strapping his leather case, the others rode up, and Bristoe, explaining the situation, set the men to making preparations for pushing on to the water-hole. Blankets were swung between ponies, and the bodies of the dead and wounded deposited therein, firm hands on the bridles. Hope rode close beside Keith, struggling to keep back the tears, as she watched him lying motionless, unconscious, scarcely breathing. So, under the early glow of the desert stars, they came to the water-hole, and halted.

The wounded man opened his eyes, and looked about him unable to comprehend. At first all was dark, silent; then he saw the stars overhead, and a breath of air fanned the near-by fire, the ruddy glow of flame flashing across his face. He heard voices faintly, and thus, little by little, consciousness asserted itself and memory struggled back into his bewildered brain. The desert — the lonely leagues of sand — his fingers gripped as if they felt the stock of a gun — yet that was all over — he was not there — but he was somewhere — and alive, alive. It hurt him to move, to breathe even, and after one effort to turn over, he lay perfectly still, staring up into the black arch of sky, endeavoring to think, to understand — where was he? How had he come there? Was Hawley alive also? A face bent over him, the features faintly visible in the flash of firelight. His dull eyes lit up in sudden recollection.

" Doc! is that you? "

" Sure, old man," the pudgy fingers feeling his pulse, the gray eyes twinkling. " Narrow squeak you had — going to pull through all right, though — no sign of fever."

" Where am I ? "

" At the water-hole; sling you in a blanket, and get you into Larned to-morrow."

There was a moment's silence, Keith finding it hard to speak.

" Hawley — ? " he whispered at last.

" Oh, don't worry; you got him all right. Say," his voice sobering, " maybe it was just as well you took that job. If it had been me I would have been in bad."

The wounded man's eyes questioned.

" It 's a bad mix-up, Keith. Waite never told us all of it. I reckon he did n't want her to know, and she never shall, if I can help it. I 've been looking over some papers in his pocket — he 'd likely been after them this trip — and his name ain't Hawley. He 's Bartlett Gale, Christie's father."

Keith could not seem to grasp the thought, his eyes half-closed.

" Her — her father? " he questioned, weakly. " Do you suppose he knew? "

" No; not at first, anyhow; not at Sheridan. He was too interested in his scheme to even suspicion he had actually stumbled onto the real girl. I think he just found out."

A coyote howled somewhere in the darkness, a melancholy chorus joining in with long-drawn cadence. A shadow swept into the radius of dancing firelight.

" Is he conscious, Doctor? "

Fairbain drew back silently, and she dropped on her knees at Keith's side, bending low to look into his face.

" Hope — Hope."

" Yes, dear, and you are going to live now — live for me."

He found her hand, and held it, clasped within his own, his eyes wide open.

"I have never told you," he said, softly, "how much I love you."

She bent lower until her cheek touched his.

"No, Jack, but you may now."

**THE END**

" It is not going to be good-bye, then.   Hope, I'll find you "